Praise for The Magic of Empowerment

"Having known Derrill since his days ⟶ in the late 1980s and following his career and accomplishments, with great enthusiasm I encourage any leader to take the time to learn as Derrill shares his life's experiences and wisdom in this wonderful and entertaining book."

—**C. Mitchell Oakley, Jr.,** Chairman, Charles Aris Inc., Fifty Years in Executive Search

"Derrill is smarter than he credits himself. His intelligence/collected experience is overridden by his tendency with humility and servant leadership approach to leadership. This skill was born with taking advantage of what seem to be slight opportunities that lead to major personal and financial gains. I gained significant insights from his business inputs while seated on the MAPP board of directors. He never shared the life journeys that I read in this book. But it made no difference. When he spoke, there was reason to listen. I assure you, this read will be worth your valuable time."

—**James Alvin Bott,** CEO, INCOE Corporation

"I had the pleasure to serve on a board with Derrill in a trade organization. This allowed me to see, in action, how he applies servant leadership with peers as well as his direct team members. It was an honor, and I am grateful to continue to learn from him through this book!"

—**Glen Fish,** CEO, Revere Plastics Systems

"This book will make you think about your own trials, tribulations, and accomplishments while also impacting the way you lead a business!"

—**Durwood Williams,** Managing
Director, Rosti North Carolina

"I had the honor of serving Derrill and his company on numerous strategic initiatives. During those interactions, I saw Derrill do exactly what he does, how he does it, and why. I learned from him every time because he's a true servant leader. He builds organizations, has fun during the process, and empowers his people. You will learn from this book and, more importantly, you will enjoy it. I know I did."

—**H. Alan Rothenbuecher,** Partner, Benesch,
Friedlander, Coplan & Aronoff LLP

"I've watched Derrill apply his servant leadership skills to a broad range of challenges across four continents and teams from dozens of different countries and cultures. While the individuals on the teams, their cultures, and the problems being solved were all very different, the outcome was always the same. This book will give you insights on how to become a servant leader that creates teams that are empowered, energized, and able to accomplish more than they ever thought was possible."

—**Steven Merkt,** President, Transportation
Solutions, TE Connectivity

"The first time I saw Derrill in action as CEO, he was working the grill at our company cookout—in humid ninety-degree heat—all while engaging with our team members and maintaining a great attitude. This story book explains why and how he does what he does!"

—**Matt Yohe,** Partner, Morgenthaler Private Equity

"I have known Derrill for almost forty years. He is the consummate business leader—poised, polished, and absolutely brilliant. We began our careers together in 1983. For over twenty years, I competed against him, worked alongside him, and reported directly to him.

"His business skills are unlimited, transcending industry and technology. I have witnessed his performance as shift manager, plant manager, sales manager, president, and CEO. Further, his scope ranges from start-up to established business, from undercapitalized businesses to those with unlimited resources. Most importantly, I am honored to call Derrill my friend."

—Mike Hargett, Partner, Barnett Bolt
Kirkwood Long Koche & Foster, PA

The MAGIC of EMPOWERMENT

The **MAGIC** of EMPOWERMENT

My Journey in
SERVANT
LEADERSHIP

J. DERRILL RICE

Advantage | Books

Published by Advantage, Charleston, South Carolina.
Member of Advantage Media.

ADVANTAGE is a registered trademark, and the Advantage colophon is a trademark of Advantage Media Group, Inc.

Printed in the United States of America.

10 9 8 7 6 5 4 3 2 1

ISBN: 978-1-64225-748-9 (Paperback)
ISBN: 978-1-64225-747-2 (eBook)

LCCN: 2023902189

Cover design by Analisa Smith.
Layout design by Lance Buckley.

This publication is designed to provide accurate and authoritative information in regard to the subject matter covered. It is sold with the understanding that the publisher is not engaged in rendering legal, accounting, or other professional services. If legal advice or other expert assistance is required, the services of a competent professional person should be sought.

Advantage Media helps busy entrepreneurs, CEOs, and leaders write and publish a book to grow their business and become the authority in their field. Advantage authors comprise an exclusive community of industry professionals, idea-makers, and thought leaders. Do you have a book idea or manuscript for consideration? We would love to hear from you at **AdvantageMedia.com**.

I dedicate this book to my grandmother, who was the anchor to my family; to my quiet-spoken grandfather, who taught me how to lay brick, pour concrete, fish, and make a living; to my father, who was there when he could be; to my mother, who was always there and sacrificed much to give me opportunities; to my wife and children, who supported me at every turn of this amazing journey; and to those known and unknown souls and special friends who impacted, enlightened, and inspired my journey.

CONTENTS

What Empowerment
MEANS TO ME

I want to start by making it clear what this book is not. This book is not about growing my personal brand. Nor is it a book about marketing my business. I am not here to "sell" you anything, so let go of any worries that this is a Trojan horse of a book that's hiding some secret sales pitch. I expect to be retiring in a few years after being blessed with a long and successful career, so I have no reason to ask anything of anyone.

But the genesis of this book came from someone asking something of *me*. About five years ago, I was first approached about discussing my philosophy of leadership by my peers and colleagues. Why? I have to assume it's because, throughout my life, people have always looked to me for my leadership. Initially, this was a big surprise to me, but from an early age, I found myself consistently being recognized for this attribute and consequently elevated to roles I never would have thought of pursuing on my own. I don't say any of this to brag (as you'll see, my personal history will bear me out on this)—but just to note that it's a talent I was lucky enough to be born with. With that innate skill as a foundation, I have been able to grow and evolve my leadership capabilities to the point where I understand what works—and what doesn't.

So when I was asked to talk about leadership, I felt honored and did a presentation about the subject. From there, I did a few more seminars, which motivated me to organize my thoughts and really think about the belief system I used in all my roles of authority. And finally, it just came to me that the secret to my success in business, as well as all the opportunities that opened up for me and the amazing journeys I've taken as a result, has all been centered around two words: *servant leadership.*

The idea of servant leadership was first articulated by business researcher Robert K. Greenleaf way back in 1964 and its central thesis is that management should serve its workers by helping them succeed in their jobs and, at the same time, be aware of their personal needs. In his book, *The Heart of Business,* former Best Buy CEO Hubert Joly summed it up very well when he wrote, "I believe that business is fundamentally about purpose, people and human relationships—not profit, at least not primarily." He goes on to say, "Doing great work for customers happens when employees relate to these customers as human beings …"[1] Your customers also benefit when you relate to those same employees as human beings and tap into their potential. It helps them, and it helps you.

It took decades for this philosophy to enter the mainstream of business thought, even though the results speak for themselves: the companies that emphasize servant leadership over profit are

---

1   Hubert Joly and Caroline Lambert, *The Heart of Business: Leadership Principles for the Next Era of Capitalism* (Boston, MA: Harvard Business Review Press, May 4, 2021).

consistently ranked at the top among their peers, with above-average results.[2]

So why do business leaders resist servant leadership when, in fact, it serves their interests so well? I cannot claim to understand why. What I do know is that the below graphic captures the concept of the inverted pyramid that represents how servant leadership works:

I'm sure you can see what's different from "business as usual" in this simple diagram. Most organizational structures put the senior person at the top and everyone else below them. Leaders at these types of operations are there to tell you what to do, and they're more than happy to micromanage you. To them, servant leadership is akin to letting the lunatics run the asylum.

---

2   Sen Sendjaya and James C. Sarros, "Servant Leadership: Its Origin, Development, and Application in Organizations," *Journal of Leadership & Organizational Studies* 9, no. 2: 57–64.

But that is not at all what servant leadership is about. It doesn't mean you're bowing down to your team and letting them take over the place. It means you're equipping your people with the tools *and* mentorship to foster a positive, productive environment that ultimately allows them (and your business) to reach their full potential.

That's why I believe my job is not to tell you what to do if you work for me. *My* job is to get hurdles out of your way so that you can be the best you can be at *your* job.

I also believe in the need to surround myself with people who are smarter than I am as well as more capable. That notion threatens some leaders, but it has actually empowered me to move among different industries throughout my career. Usually, when you make it to a very senior level, you get pigeonholed within that business sector. In other words, if you rise to the top of a construction company, you tend to stay in construction. But because I'm not afraid to rely on other people's expertise, that hasn't happened to me. The last job I had, where I was president, CEO, and on the company's board of directors, was at a thermoplastic injection molding company. Now, if you asked me about how exactly that technology worked … well, I would have sent you to someone who could answer that question, because I sure couldn't!

At a leadership level, I only need to know … well, what I need to know. In my first job at a textile plant, I sure as heck learned how to set up a weaving machine and run a tenter frame. That was part of my job. But as a CEO, my job is not to be the best engineer. My job is to make sure that those who are engineers have the tools they need to succeed.

That last sentence represents an idea I believe is the key to servant leadership—*empowerment.* That's the conclusion I came to as I mentally reviewed all the pivotal points of my life. I succeeded when I was either empowered by someone else or I empowered myself. In turn, I saw good outcomes in all my relationships, personal and professional, when I was able to empower others.

According to Oxford Languages, the definition of empowerment is "authority or power given to someone to do something." Empowerment goes beyond that, however. When you empower someone, you demonstrate trust and respect in the other person, as well as their ability to handle responsibility. Most people appreciate that and will work their butts off to live up to your faith in them—with the result being they improve their own skill set and attitude in the process. I have been the happy recipient of that type of empowerment. Great mentoring empowered me to lead several businesses in multiple industries from $30 million to $1.2 billion in size, with my amazing family always providing me with incredible support along the way.

I'm aware there are thousands of business memoirs out there offering their own unique definitions of what success is and how to achieve it. This, however, is mine. In the pages to come, I will be sharing a lot of stories of how empowerment allowed me—and others in my life—to achieve at a high level. Some of it will almost seem magical … but that might just be because I'm a real magician (if you think I'm joking, wait till I tell you how I made a car disappear from the center stage of an auditorium in front of the one and only Edsel Ford II). But I do believe you will see how empowerment has been central to everything I've gotten out of life, and it can be for you as well.

I appreciate your taking the time to read this book and hope it offers you some practical advice on how leadership can lift people up rather than keep them down.

CHAPTER 1

Early

EMPOWERMENT

No one needs empowerment more than a child.

Kids need to know they've got someone on their side from an early age, someone who has faith in their talents and abilities and is willing to entrust them with the responsibility to use them wisely. That's how they develop self-confidence right from the start, as well as the motivation to want to do a job right.

I was one of those fortunate kids, because my mother always made it a point to empower me to succeed.

One way she did that was to make sure there was only one Derrill in the world—me. I'm not being egotistical about this; the plain fact is the name was her invention. My grandfather was James Alvin Rice, his son (my father) was James Alvin Rice Jr., and I was supposed to be James Alvin Rice III. My mother was dead set against that—however, she was very fond of the name Derek. So the compromise was that Derek would be somehow mushed together with Alvin to create (with a few extra letters) Derrill, which my mom encouraged me to use as my main name. I did just that, using the initial *J* at the front, standing for *James*. It gets confusing at times, going by my middle name, but, on the other hand, when I'm signing up for an online account or something like that, I can be sure I won't be competing with any other Derrills for a username—because I'm the only one.

I grew up without a father as a part of my daily life. The story was he had bipolar disorder, a mental condition that wasn't really dealt with back then, and his severe mood swings made for a very unstable relationship with my mother. I was told that's why, when I was five, my grandfather came and spirited me and my younger brother away from where we lived in Virginia and took me on the train down to Georgia, where he and my grandmother lived. My mother followed in the morning. I was too young to remember much of this.

Mom became a government civil service employee at nearby Fort Benning, the largest infantry base in the country at the time. She divorced my dad and now faced the daunting challenge of raising two active boys on her own. Although my grandparents supported our family in every way they could, we still lived in a very poor part of town, and paying the monthly bills was an ongoing challenge for us. Although I would still see my dad twice a year, at Christmas and during the summer, sometimes a couple of years would go by when I wouldn't hear from him. And I never knew of his mental health issues until he passed away and his brother (my uncle) filled me in on some of what he went through. The tragedy of his life was that he was born before a condition like his could really be effectively medicated.

The blessing in his life, however, was that he was still able to do great things, such as starting his own auto businesses. He eventually married a loving woman with two daughters whom he cared for as if they were his own. Although the Lord took him at an early age when he suffered a fatal heart attack at fifty-four, he finished life strong, in a good place, and with a wonderful family.

The Whirling Dervish of Dishwashers

As I indicated, money was tight for our little family. I did what I could to help out my mom. I had paper routes and would do odd jobs like mowing the neighbor's lawn. Clearly, however, we needed something more substantial to add to our monthly income.

This led to me getting the job I enjoyed more than any other over my lifetime—as a dishwasher.

I'm aware most—if not all—people who have worked as dishwashers definitely would not remember their duties so fondly. But this was my first "adult" job (I was twelve when I started) and, as you'll see, I definitely made the most of it. In a way, through this job, I learned how I could empower myself to excel.

What happened was my mother knew the owner of the local Shakey's Pizza Parlor. She asked him to give me a shot, and he agreed. First, I had to go to the county and get a work permit, since they served beer on the premises and I was very far from reaching the age to legally drink. Fortunately, the permit was granted, and so I showed up for work.

> Through this job, I learned how I could empower myself to excel.

Now, this was a time before there was any industrial dishwashing equipment—I had to do everything by hand. And on Friday and Saturday night, that was quite the challenge. There were three large wells lined up in the dishwashing area—the first was filled with hot water and soap for washing, the second with hot water and no soap for rinsing, and the third one just contained cold water for a final cooling rinse. To the side of the wells was the drying area for the dishes.

There was only one problem with this system, and it was a big one—I was still too short for it to work! I had to build makeshift stools to stand on in order to reach into the wells with the dishes so I could wash them. And since there were three wells, I had to set up three stools, one for each well, so I could move fast enough from one to another. In a way, I didn't feel as though I had a choice. On Friday and Saturday nights, the place was packed, and I had to keep things moving or we would run out of clean dishes. I didn't intend to disappoint.

So imagine a twelve-year-old boy jumping as fast as possible from stool to stool with a brush that was almost as big as he was. That was me. I was moving like the Tasmanian Devil, a blur of motion, and the staff marveled at how fast I jumped up on the stools and back down, bouncing back and forth between the wells, washing dishes faster than anyone there had ever seen before. On any one of those weekend nights, I would always end up a big soapy soaking-wet mess by the end of my shift. I guess I put on quite a show—the owner would actually bring customers into the kitchen just to watch me do my thing!

I don't tell this story to brag about my dishwashing skills, which, to be honest, are probably no longer up to the standard I set back then. I tell it because the experience taught me an invaluable lesson: *if you do a great job, to the best of your ability, people will notice and admire and respect you for your effort.* I loved the recognition I received and enjoyed working there so much that, during the summers, the owner and I made a deal: I could work as many hours as I wanted as long as I never charged overtime!

By the time I was sixteen, I was the store manager on the weekends during the school year and, during the summers, due to that aforementioned deal, I sometimes worked eighty hours a week, working there from open to close every day. The hours didn't kill me, but something else almost did. One Saturday morning, I was there by myself and mixing together all the dough in a big metal mixing bowl, when I accidentally pushed the bowl against an exposed and worn 220-volt power cord connected to the meat grinder. Suddenly, my whole body was shaking like it was made of Jell-O, and I fell to the floor, where I remained out cold for a solid half hour. The lucky part was that I had inadvertently pulled the metal bowl away from the power cord when the shock first hit me, and that probably saved my life.

It was adversity that motivated my mom to get me that job at the age of twelve, but I still think it was one of the greatest things that ever happened to me. Aside from almost being electrocuted and getting the occasional burn marks on the sides of my arms from pulling hot pizzas out of the ovens, I had a lot of fun—all of us working there did. Customers could see into the kitchen through its surrounding windows, so, dressed in red aprons and wearing plastic Shakey's hats, we would put on a show. For example, I would create smiley faces with pepperoni on the pizza tops to the joy of the football team cheerleaders looking in to see what I was up to. I would also literally hurl a pizza pie like a Frisbee, launching it from the oven to the cutting table. We worked hard and laughed loud as we got the job done with high spirits, and then celebrated when it was the end of a hard and busy weekend night.

And that taught me yet another valuable early life lesson. *If you love your work, if you enjoy it, you will be motivated to be good at it.* I never asked to be promoted in this first professional experience—I was simply asked to take on more and more responsibility over the years, and I stepped up accordingly.

I don't believe you can be great at a job you hate. Passion provides a special kind of personal empowerment, and that's something I never forgot.

Magic: An Unintended Detour, A Lifetime Gift

The tricky thing about passion, however, is that you can't really control what just might get your engine going. That's why it can take you down some unexpected paths, paths that might seem silly or a waste of time to others. But, again, you have to respect where your heart leads you—and in my case, it was magic. Maybe putting on a dishwashing show for the pizza parlor every weekend had given me the showbiz bug, but suddenly, doing magic was my obsession, an obsession that would pay off big in unexpected ways both as a teenager as well as years and years later.

It started when I rode the bus I had to take on weekdays, from the poor part of town where we lived to the rich part of town where I went to school (more on that later). About halfway through that ride, this other boy named Court Hamlet would get on board, and we started to hang out, because we were two of the older kids, around fifteen at the time. So we would sit in the back of the bus and play cards.

Those cards gave me an idea.

Cut back to the pizza parlor. There was a fellow employee there who walked with a limp and hinted at some shadiness in his past. He would often tell stories about his gambling. I guess I began to wonder if he had any secrets to share, so one day, I flat-out asked him, "Can you teach me how to deal from the bottom of the deck?" He agreed; I picked it up quickly, and I tried the trick out on Court the next time we played cards. I had it down.

A week or so later, the guy returned to the pizza parlor and offered to show me a few more tricks, including how to make something I was holding look like it had vanished into thin air, often called *close-up magic*. I was fascinated. I would sit at home in front of a mirror and practice what he taught me, watching my reflection closely so I could see if the intended visual effects of the tricks really worked.

I got Court into magic as well, but he ended up losing interest after we put on what was probably the worst magic show ever at the summer camp where we went to school. I think the audience wanted us to disappear. I wasn't deterred, however. I stayed with it and started working birthday parties and other occasions. My tricks grew more sophisticated, and the money I made from my shows enabled me to buy more equipment for my tricks. Eventually, one summer I was hired to do magic shows Thursday nights at Callaway Gardens, a big resort with a lake in nearby Pine Mountain. I had a live band behind me and everything. And I learned how to manage a crowd. One time I messed up a trick and quickly recovered from my embarrassment—by swearing the audience to secrecy, telling them that if the International Brotherhood of Magicians found out about my mistake, they'd boot me out (yes, it is a real organization, but I sincerely doubt they had agents out there monitoring my performances). I then did the trick correctly and probably got about twice the response from the crowd as I would've without screwing it up the first time around.

As I said, I began to collect more and more equipment for my shows, so much so that I had to lug my stuff around in a small U-Haul trailer to every gig. I also put an outdoor bird cage in the backyard where I could keep doves for the act, which I continued doing all through college. Why not? I continued to love it—and it actually paid good money! I stopped only because my postcollege jobs were just too demanding (although I still did an extremely scaled-down act at rest homes or a church event from time to time—no U-Haul, just a briefcase!).

For me, magic was fascinating for two reasons.

First, it challenged my technology and math skills—once I built a box from scratch that enabled my future wife (she served as my assistant for a few gigs) and myself to seemingly switch places instantly, and it always got a standing ovation. Now, I didn't have any instructions on how to create this illusion—I just saw a magician do it once and thought through what he had to do to make the trick work. Turned out I guessed right.

Second, it taught me how to interact with a crowd. A magic act doesn't work if you can't entertain people and tell a great story with your illusions. That came in handy later on when, as a business leader, I would have to present to a lot of people. So I came away from my little magical detour with a few new tricks of my own. And yet, I wouldn't perform my biggest trick until years later. More on that to come.

Before I leave the subject of magic, I want to be clear about something. I never thought magic would actually be my career—that just didn't seem practical to me at all. It was a cool hobby that could actually earn me money—and that was a great combination for me at the time. It wouldn't have worked for me if it hadn't been fun and I hadn't enjoyed it. And it kept me a whole lot dryer than my old dishwashing duties had.

Highs and Lows

As I said, my mom empowered me at an early age. Her confidence in me helped me feel secure enough to take chances I maybe wouldn't have otherwise, so that when the right doors opened up in front of me, I didn't hesitate to walk through them. This was a gift I wanted to give my own kids. So when I began having children of my own, I wanted them to grow up feeling empowered as well.

To me, raising a new generation required a strategic plan, a tactical map, an escape plan, and a whole lot more! As all you parents reading this know, kids require a lot of work, but I wanted their journey into adulthood to be as fun and productive as mine was. When our daughter,

Caroline, and son, Austin, were born, my wife, Lori (whom I'll properly introduce to you later), took charge of their journeys from day one. As an acclaimed educator who has taught all kinds of children on two different continents, she was well equipped to challenge them in all the right ways and didn't shrink from that duty.

And by the way, she challenged them even before they were born! I remember being directed by her to speak into a tube that ended in a funnel placed across her pregnant belly. Evidently, this was to help my soon-to-be daughter recognize my voice after birth. Does this sound crazy? It did to me at the time. And do not even get me started about how she insisted on using

> When I began having children of my own, I wanted them to grow up feeling empowered.

flash cards on them when they were only three months old. With an undergraduate in education, a master's degree in gifted education, and later on achieving a lower and upper elementary Montessori teacher certification, she was focused on empowering our children with a great start in life. And today she teaches teachers in two state programs. She was and is an amazing educator!

Dinner became an all-important time for us, one of the few times during the week that all of us could sit down together and interact. To keep that interaction front and center, we allowed no cell phones, no TV, no music, and no other distractions so that we were all truly *present*.

As soon as our kids sat down with us around the dinner table, my wife would kick things off with what we called the *High/Low Drill*. Everyone had to answer the question "What was your high point and low point of the day?" This didn't always go smoothly—sometimes, Caroline would add a "medium" point ... or Austin would refuse to share a "low" because he just wanted to forget about whatever had happened—but things rarely go as scripted with kids. But this was no arbitrary exercise—it was a way we could all connect with each other in person and face to face and share our various challenges and triumphs. Most of all, it required us to focus on communication and bonding as a family.

Another parenting concern of mine was that, in a way, I *had* to be motivated as a kid. We didn't have much, and I felt obligated to help the family out. When I became a father, however, I was on a much more solid financial footing. Would my kids really appreciate the value of a dollar and how hard it was to earn one? I came up with a plan that would both empower them to practice financial responsibility while still allowing me to contribute to their efforts. So when they wanted something beyond a birthday or Christmas present, I made a deal with them—we would split the cost. They could earn the money by doing chores around the house, getting a job, or working with me on some special project. I had a notebook where they could keep track of what they earned, and when they were ready to buy whatever they were after at the time, I'd deduct half the cost from what they had earned, and I'd pay for the other half.

We kept that system going all the way to the point when they bought their first cars as well as paid half their college tuition, allowing them to attend more expensive schools than they otherwise would have. What that also did was give them skin in the game. I believed that if they had to bear half the cost, it would motivate them to take their higher education more seriously.

We also didn't allow the kids to get any tattoos until they had a job and could pay for them. Caroline was the first—and Lori got her first tattoo at the same time! On each wrist, Caroline had tattooed, "A bushel and a peck," and Lori's says, "And a hug around the neck." This was a childhood saying—"I love you a bushel and a peck and a hug around the neck." Austin got one not too long after and, believe it or not, I got a couple of my own! On my left shoulder is the captain's insignia from the original *Star Trek* series, worn by Captain James T. Kirk himself. And on my right shoulder is the USS *Enterprise*. When I tell people about the two tattoos on either shoulder, I add, "And in between is your captain." (Yes, I am a Trekkie, and I believe the *Star Trek* creator Gene Roddenberry was a visionary—I would pretend that my first Motorola flip phone was just like the *Star Trek* communicator, although Scotty never answered to beam me up, sadly …).

To sum up, I believe you empower your children in three ways: (1) by being present for them, (2) by showing interest in their lives, and (3) by finding ways to make them self-motivated people through empowerment. The good thing is I feel as though we pulled off that hat trick. Today, both of them are very successful. Caroline is a New York University (NYU) graduate who just started her own branding and strategy business focused on the hospitality industry in Denver, while Austin is a Lehigh University graduate and a systems engineer for Boeing at its facility in Seattle. And even though our kids are now young adults, we still do the High/Low Drill when we're together as a family. I hope they pass that tradition on to their children.

There is no question an empowered child has the best chance of successfully navigating adulthood. They have already discovered how to push themselves forward and acquire the tools they need to make their way out in the world, and now they're contributing to make it a better place!

The author James Allen once wrote, "The oak sleeps in the acorn." Treat the acorn right, and that oak will grow to be a tall, mighty tree.

C H A P T E R   2

Empowered by
OPPORTUNITY

*The kingdom of heaven is like a mustard seed, which a man took
and planted in his field. Though it is the smallest of all seeds,
yet when it grows, it is the largest of garden plants and becomes
a tree, so that the birds come and perch in its branches.*

That famous parable is from Matthew 13:31–32. In my younger years, that analogy could have applied directly to me. Because I didn't come from a lot of money, I did indeed feel like the "smallest of seeds." And I was far from sure that I would end up growing to be a tree.

What made the difference in my life was *opportunity*. When I was fortunate enough to be presented with the right one, I generally didn't blink. I dove right in and worked to take advantage of it as much as I could—even when I was doubtful that I was capable of what was being asked of me! I learned early on that the only way you can be truly empowered when someone opens a door of opportunity on your behalf … is to actually walk through that door and work as hard as possible to make it pay off. That's what I did with my first dishwashing job, and that's what I did as I moved forward into my teenage years.

The legendary inventor Thomas Edison once said, "Opportunity is missed by most people because it is dressed in overalls and looks like work." There's a lot of wisdom in that statement.

Brookstone

My mother knew that in order for her kids to have the best opportunity to succeed in life, the right education was going to be essential. So she wanted to make sure my younger brother and I were placed in an academic atmosphere that would allow us to thrive. And she knew, as I approached the age for middle school, that the local option would not be the right one.

That's because the area high school at the time had a bad reputation, as well as a dangerous one. We would hear of stabbings happening on campus. My mom didn't think that kind of school would set me up properly for college (if I lived to graduate, that is!). Luckily, my grades had been excellent, so, through a lot of hard work, I was able to get an academic scholarship to Brookstone, a small private school at the north end of town. I don't know if my life would have worked out as well if I hadn't been given this great opportunity, as Brookstone allowed this mustard seed to blossom in a way that might not have happened elsewhere.

> Brookstone School helped prepare me for the next chapters in my journey.

The beginning wasn't easy, however. When I began attending classes at Brookstone in the seventh grade, I didn't know a soul among my new classmates—and making connections at first was difficult.

The school was located in a much more affluent area than where we lived, so I didn't exactly fit in with the "rich kids," and they knew it. They had already bonded as a group, as most had been together on a high-level academic trajectory since kindergarten. Here I was, a complete outsider popping up out of nowhere, which is probably where they thought I should have stayed. Yes, the teachers were professional, accomplished, and nice—I learned a lot from them. But entering this whole new world was a shock to my system.

One bright spot. I did make one friend in seventh grade, Tim Wilson. Tim was from a similar background as mine, so we were very comfortable with each other. As a matter of fact, the first time I stayed over at a friend's house was at his place. Tim had two siblings and a mom and dad, so their family was a bit bigger than mine. At dinnertime, I watched in amazement as his mom brought out bowls full of food and, after the blessing, all conversation immediately stopped as the whole family started eating so furiously it seemed like they hadn't had a meal in a week. I suddenly realized I'd better start keeping up with them or I'd go hungry.

That night, Tim said to me, "Let's go to the store down the street." Question marks were in my eyes because I was not sure of the mission, but of course I went with him. We walked in with our stories straight—"Mom said, get eggs and milk, right?" Tim yelled to me as we entered. So we walked out with a dozen eggs and a milk jug. We immediately threw out the milk and headed to the local school playground. After throwing a few eggs at the swing set and monkey bars, I was thinking that this adventure was kind of boring. Little did I know how fast things would change. Tim saw car lights coming down the lower street. Under his direction, we launched a couple of eggs.

It was quiet. As they say in the Westerns, "too quiet." A shadow appeared after a couple of minutes, and we heard a deep voice yelling at us: "You damn boys throwing eggs!" We didn't stick around for whatever else he was going to say (or do); instead, we ran off, hearing dogs bark as we ran into the night. Suddenly, we were convinced that we were being hunted, like we were convicts who'd just busted out of the lockup. Crazed with adrenaline and fear, we ran through some woods that were packed with briars and emerged with half those briars sticking to us. We finally came out by a street and suddenly were blinded by the lights of a car headed our way. As it pulled over, we had to hope it wasn't carrying some kind of posse hastily assembled to track down egg-throwing delinquents. The person getting out of the car, fortunately, was Tony, Tim's older brother, coming to our rescue—only he didn't know it. He had no idea what we were up to; he just saw us and decided to give us a ride. He didn't ask why we were covered with briars and why we looked so shaken up—he just took us back to Tim's place.

It wasn't until years later that I found out how Tim had gone over to the house where the car we had egged was parked and cleaned up the mess himself. Why would he chance that? When I look back on it, I can see that Tim was just a good person and held himself accountable for his actions. He became a lifetime friend—a brother solidified not by blood but by friendship.

Tim was an amazing personality. He became a singer/songwriter (I learned guitar just so I could back him up), a stand-up comic, and a local radio celebrity, and he even ended up guesting on *The Tonight Show with Jay Leno*. Tim also wrote and recorded music (he's in the Georgia Music Hall of Fame) and put out over a dozen comedy albums. Unfortunately, he passed away long before his time, partly because of the tough lifestyle he had created for himself as an entertainer—he chain-smoked and didn't mind his health as maybe he should have. But because of his achievements, he received the Distinguished Alumni Award from Brookstone High School posthumously. His younger sister Lynn accepted it on his behalf at the school's homecoming event that year, and I had the honor of presenting his life journey to the crowd. As you will see throughout this book, Tim had a major impact on my life—including introducing me to my wife!

Back to Brookstone. The school expected a lot of its students. Since it was designed as a prep school to prepare kids for higher education, its curriculum was rigorous and aggressive. That was fine with me. I've never been afraid of hard work, so I put my head down and focused on my studies. In the process, I quickly established myself as a heavyset nerd, which also didn't do much for my popularity. Luckily, academics came easy to me, even here. Athletics was another thing, however. As I indicated, I wasn't exactly svelte when I started at Brookstone, and because of my afterschool work schedule, I never had time to play team sports or develop any athletic skills beyond what I gained from a few karate classes my mom encouraged me to take to develop my physicality. So I stuck to academics.

That was all about to radically change—because of Tim.

Friday Night Lights

I wasn't enjoying my "brand" as the school's heavyset nerd, so one day, I decided to start getting rid of all my extra weight. Brookstone's resources came to the rescue. Since anybody could use the school gym, I worked out there three times a week, doing mostly weightlifting. Gradually, the fat transformed to muscle, and my new gym-rat ways began to pay off. People began to notice my new physique. I had unwittingly set myself up for a new opportunity, but it only came to fruition because of Tim.

Unbeknownst to me, Tim, using his gregarious and outgoing personality, had become a kind of advance man for me during my sophomore year. He was going around setting me up for two larger-than-life opportunities with the other students. That effort culminated in two big football players, one a quarterback and the other a running back from my class, coming up to me in the hallway and asking me to do two things I never would have considered on my own.

"First of all, there's nobody in the rising senior class that has any leadership skills, so you need to run for student body president as a rising junior."

President? Me? Oh. Okay.

"Second, we need more people on the football team. You should join up."

Football team? Sure. Why not?

Many people would have listened to those two directives and walked away shaking their heads. Not me. If I really had the support of these two big dogs, there were a couple more doors of opportunity I wanted to walk through.

The bigger challenge, running for the highest office at the school, turned out to be the easier one. Incredibly, I won the school election and became student body president as a junior, which was unheard of (and still is at that high school and many others as well).

The smaller challenge, joining the football team, turned out to be the tougher ask. My mom was dead set against me playing. Even back then, football was regarded as a dangerous sport, and she didn't want me hurt. That's where Windle McKenzie was a game changer. Mr. McKenzie was my high school math teacher, and since math was one of my favorite subjects, we already had a bond. But he didn't just teach math—he also coached the football team and was keen on having me on it. With that goal in mind, he actually drove out to our house to talk to my mother privately. He reassured her that he would be looking out for me if she should allow me to play. At least, that's what I *think* he said; I never found out any details of the actual conversation. Whatever he said, it worked, and my mom said yes.

That led to another unlikely moment in my life—the very first time I ever saw a football game live. I say "unlikely" because I was playing in that game as a starting linebacker!

I found I loved everything about football—even the uphill sprints at the end of practice. I was a starting linebacker from the beginning, and later, as a senior, I was named captain of the defense. A big appeal of the sport was that it actually played into my mathematic skills as well. Football to me is real-time math—you've got the different offensive versus defensive setups, you've got anticipation of a play, and you have to figure out how to minimize the other team's ability to make progress. So I was able to use my mental skills as well as my newfound physical ones.

I also made some friends for life, one of them being David Spitzmiller. Middle linebackers have a partner on most lineups. David was my partner—we called him Mue. David was a senior, and I was a junior and, on campus, there is always a real divide between upper and lower classmen. But that made no difference when the clock was running on the field—it was a matter of your skills and determination, not your social status. A great team empowers you, a theme I will continue to return to throughout this book. And sometimes someone special brings a higher level of empowerment to the experience. For me, that someone special was David, who inspired me to play better football and learn the true spirit of the game.

David had a gift for reading the offense. And he had a passion for football like no other. After the huddle, as we approached the line of scrimmage, David instinctively read the offense. With a blink of an eye or a nod of the head he telegraphed the plan, whether I would blitz, he would blitz, we both would blitz or drop back or go to the left or to the right … well, you get the drill. And so did I, eventually. The coaching staff taught me the *what* about football, but David taught me the *how*. I valued him as a teammate, and I value him to this day as a friend. A half century later and we're still in touch.

Now, what about my mom, you might be asking. Well, she came to see every game, watching me play with a constant low level of panic. As for those fears of hers about me getting hurt? Well, they ended up being a bit justified.

We were playing the team from Hogansville, which at the time represented a mountain we had to climb. They had a lightning-fast tailback who managed to grab the ball during almost every play. Once he broke the line of scrimmage, he was unstoppable. So our coaching staff developed a unique defensive strategy—a 6–1 front line. Six linemen filled every gap on the line of scrimmage except the guard/tackle gap on each side of the center. There was one linebacker lined up on the center—me. My job was simple—keep my eyes on the helmet of that superfast tailback. At the snap, his head would move left or right. My charge was to blindly shoot the guard/tackle gap in the direction of the head move. We knew we could not let him get past the line of scrimmage, and Coach McKenzie was relentless on me in practice, emphasizing that I had to move when that tailback's helmet did.

And that's what I did. On the very first play, the tailback's head moved to the right, and I shot the gap. The result resembled two freight trains colliding. All I remember is two of my teammates, Jim Eaton and Tim Tarpley, pulling me off the grass with head butts and butt slaps, as they said over and over, "Great job, Rice—way to stop him in his tracks!" And that was the *last* thing I remember from that game. I must have suffered a slight concussion. I say *slight* because, somehow, I played the rest of the game, even though I still to this day have no memory of it. But I would soon have a detailed—and very unexpected—record of it.

First thing the next morning, my coach called and told me to go buy a copy of the *Atlanta Journal-Constitution* newspaper. When I did so, I was stunned, and this time not from getting my brains scrambled the night before. I had made the cover of the sports sections, with a picture of me on the field and everything! The article stated I had made seventeen unassisted tackles and three assisted tackles—a Georgia state record that had snapped Hogansville's long winning streak. Yes, it was my best game ever. I just wish I could remember it.

There was one other incident, and it happened when we were training for a spring practice game. A player's helmet slammed directly into my wrist with such force that it lifted me off the ground. The pain was excruciating, and I thought I definitely had a bad sprain, if not a break. But I kept playing, making sure to protect my right arm to the extent that I even used my left arm for the down position. After the game, the coach looked at my wrist and put it on ice, and by Friday, the swelling started going down. Our spring preseason game against a local rival, Pachelli Catholic, was that night—it would be my first as captain, and there was no way I was going to miss it, wrist or no wrist. Before the game, they taped it up and put on an arm brace to protect it. I got through the game, and we won. I decided when Monday rolled around, I would get it checked by a doctor. That never happened, because by then, the wrist stopped hurting, even though I still couldn't bend it all the way back.

A couple of years later, when I was in college, the wrist was still bothering me, and I finally sought some medical advice. That's when X-rays revealed that I had broken a bone there. Not only that, but the bone had been broken for so long with no blood supply to keep it healthy that it had actually disintegrated. The doctors just sanded off what was left, so I was left with a permanent scar and a missing bone. It's never slowed me down; it's just a little inconvenient.

So let's get back to opportunities. I often think to myself, "What if I had handled that moment in the school hallway when the two football players recruited me for their team as well as student body president differently?" I could have laughed in their faces and walked away. Or I could have politely turned them down and told them there was no way either thing could happen for me.

And I would have missed out on a lot of amazing outcomes.

I had entered a school where I felt like a stranger in a strange land because I didn't know anyone. And I ended up becoming the captain of the football team as well as twice-president of the student body (I was also reelected for my senior year, making me the only two-time student body president and valedictorian in the school's history to this date). It all happened because I had taken advantage of opportunities that came my way. Just having a gym available to me for free at the school was a gift I happily accepted.

> Though at Brookstone, I found some pretty fertile ground for my mustard seed to grow.

Maybe some of this would have still happened if I had gone to the local school. Who knows? The strange part for me is, while I had gotten so much out of the Brookstone experience, I still thought of myself as odd man out while I went there. Those feelings felt in the distant past as I attended our recent fortieth reunion. Although I was not afforded the opportunity in school to participate in many of the social activities, I was welcomed by my former classmates as a friend and just another member of the class of 1979. I felt as though at Brookstone, I found some pretty fertile ground for my mustard seed to grow.

A Weighty Decision

I want to skip ahead a few years and tell one more story about another completely random opportunity that I was given and ran with. It didn't change up my life in a major way, but it brought an extra dimension to my everyday life that ended up being a lot of fun.

As I already said, I lifted weights in high school. Well, that was an activity I kept on doing, even after I became a family man and a working man. For me, a powerlifting gym was a very special place. Why? Well, not because of the chalk powder on the bars and on the floor. And not because of the loud rock and roll music. It wasn't because of the clanging sounds of iron slamming against iron, the smell of ammonia, or the intense yells and screams coming from lifters. I loved all those elements of the atmosphere, to be sure, but what I most loved about the gym was that everybody who was there couldn't care less about what you did outside the gym. All that mattered was what you did *inside* it. It was a perfect escape—I could clear my mind of day-to-day reality and work on my mission to stay strong.

This particular story happened when I was in my early thirties. I had just moved to a small community for my job (more on that later), and I needed a place for my Monday/Wednesday/Friday one-hour lifting sessions. However, because the town was so small, my options were very limited. I finally chose a small weights-only powerlifting gym conveniently located near my house, which provided a key code that gave members twenty-four-hour access. Perfect. And again, I loved the fact that nobody gave a hang about who I was or what I did for a living. Heck, I probably worked out there for five years before anybody even knew that I was president of the largest company in town because my title and position were irrelevant. It didn't matter. All that mattered was that I pushed weight and worked to make myself better in the gym.

Then I got noticed.

One Monday night, I was in the gym quietly doing my routine and minding my own business, as I always did. Whenever I went to lift, I would just finish my routine and get the heck out of there. I wasn't the only regular on that night, however. Mondays, there was always a group of three big bruisers in the left corner of the gym tossing around big plates and pressing some major pounds on the bench press.

These guys were the living embodiment of testosterone. They would yell at each other. They would chest-butt. They would chest-slap. They would take a big whiff of ammonia, tighten their waist belts one last time, and then press an enormous amount of poundage, after which there would be a short (and of course loud) celebration complete with high fives. I would look over at them and smile. Yeah, they were intense as all get-out, but they also seemed to be having an amazing time!

Well, that Monday night, as I positioned myself on another bench to get in the last set of my bench routine, someone jumped on the step at the head of the bench, grabbed the bar, and said, "Hey, man, I'll give you a lift off, and then give you a spot so you can rep to exhaustion." It was one of the bruisers. I thanked the guy and did my lift.

Afterward, this guy asked me how much I weighed and what my single-rep bench press maximum was. I answered, and he turned to a fellow bruiser and yelled, "THIS IS WHAT WE'VE BEEN LOOKING FOR!"

Me? For what reason?

I was hoping I didn't resemble somebody on the FBI most wanted list or something, because frankly, I had no idea what he was talking about. I had never really interacted with these guys much.

I was always in my own quiet little world, and they were always in their much louder one.

What I found out was these bruisers (yes, they did have names—Robin, Todd, Tim, and Grey, the gym owner and an accomplished body builder) had a bench press meet coming up in a month, and they needed a bencher in the 181-weight class to complete the team. I fit the bill. I tried to explain to them that I had never competed in this sport, this was just how I kept in shape, but they didn't care. They had been watching me for the past month or so and were convinced I had the goods to become a competitive powerlifter. Sure, they had to teach me a few things, but they were sure I could do it.

Yes, I was once again empowered by an unexpected opportunity.

This led to an incredible discovery—this little unassuming gym was really a big deal in the lifting universe. It had produced a long list of champions who had competed at the World Powerlifting competition in Helsinki, Finland, as well as the Arnold Strongman Classic (named for you know who). I was at the epicenter of powerlifting greatness!

My family, however, wasn't used to the powerlifting culture. When my wife came to see me at my first meet, she didn't like it when Todd slapped me as hard as he could on my chest to give me an adrenaline hit right before I had to perform. After the meet, she walked up to Todd and told him, "Don't you ever hit my husband like that again!" You gotta love that.

I found powerlifting to be extremely empowering, because it's more about competing against yourself as opposed to other lifters. Like a marathon runner trying to better their personal best on the time clock, a lifter tries to better *their* personal best lift or, at least, better the results from the last competition. I enjoyed challenging myself, it was great to get the constant (and, yes, loud) support from the other guys, and, just like with football, I ended up doing quite well with my new powerlifting hobby. So much so that in my late forties, I won the title for drug-free powerlifters at the bench press national meet in Nashville, Tennessee. I went on to set a personal best regulation press with a pause single lift of 430 pounds and set several national records as well.

Powerlifting often builds lifetime friendships, and it certainly did in this case. The bruisers and I still lift together when schedules permit, which isn't as often as I would like, but that's life.

Opportunities don't have to be about education or jobs or anything all that important. Sometimes, they can just open up a fun new pastime you don't even know exists. Actually, it became more than a pastime—it's now more of a life journey. I still work out almost every day with Robin, a friend of mine for some thirty years. Yes, the weights we work with are much lighter, because we are now "old men," and heavy lifting at this point is just a memory. Now, just getting to the gym is more than half the battle!

Empowered by
EDUCATION

The value of higher education is undeniable.

You probably already know that college graduates earn more than those who only completed high school. According to Pew Research, in 2021, full-time workers between the ages of twenty-two and twenty-seven with a bachelor's degree made a median annual wage of $52,000, versus $30,000 for those who only held a high school diploma, a difference of $22,000. That's a gap that's only growing larger. Back in 1990, those numbers were $48,481 for college grads versus $35,257, a difference of roughly $13,000.

(To me, this difference is exacerbated by the lack of a technical/industrial career path option in school. Shop classes in high schools and community colleges have been eliminated. The option to develop a career as an electrician or plumber is more difficult due to a lack of access to such education. I know plumbers and electricians who have built great businesses and have very rewarding lifestyles. Now, we are facing a generation gap in technical talent from journeyman tool makers to car mechanics and setup technicians.)

It's also easier to get a job if you have a college degree. In February of 2020, just before COVID-19 hit, only 1.9 percent of college graduates twenty-five and older were unemployed, compared to 3.7 percent of workers with only a high school diploma.

Finally, being a college grad also tends to pay off for your kids. When it comes to income and wealth accumulation, first-generation college graduates lag substantially behind those with college-educated parents, who are able to pass on more generational wealth.

It's not all about money and jobs either. Most Americans with college degrees feel as though they've gained a lot of value just from the experience. Pew Research has shown that 79 percent of college grads felt their education was extremely or very useful in terms of helping them grow personally and intellectually.[3]

Personally, there was never a question of me going on to college from Brookstone. There was only the question of how I would be able to afford it. I knew that I needed a degree to get the kind of job and have the kind of life I wanted. But I also knew I would have to work like crazy to get that degree.

Higher education would empower my life. I knew that, and I was determined to avail myself of it. Luckily, there were people along the way who helped me reach my goal.

Making My Way

The college I chose was Presbyterian College in Clinton, South Carolina, because they offered the best academic financial support package

---

3   Katherine Schaeffer, *10 Facts about Today's College Graduates*, Pew Research Center, April 12, 2022, https://www.pewresearch.org/fact-tank/2022/04/12/10-facts-about-todays-college-graduates/.

compared to competing institutions (and it was only a four-hour drive from home). Even with that support, however, I still had to work between thirty and forty hours a week to pay for the rest of my tuition and expenses. That meant that my football career was over—I just would not have the time to devote to the team that was required.

Instead, I got a job with a landscaping company that was known for hiring college kids. My classes were usually over after lunch (except for lab days), which meant I was free to work there from one to six every day, mowing lawns, planting bushes, all the usual lawn jobs.

Still, I wanted to have the social experience as well as the academic challenge that college offered. After freshman orientation, there was a huge "Welcome Back" party for all the upperclassmen. After my high school triumphs, I was feeling as though that party would be my first step toward conquering this campus as well. So I showered, shaved, and dressed to impress, and I headed to the Student Center for the big night. The party was cranking, and everyone was doing a dance called the Carolina Shag. I had never seen this dance before in my life, so I instantly felt out of place. Not only that, but as soon as people found out I was a freshman, nobody wanted to connect with me! The women were all focused on the older guys, and I was left out in the cold. Depressed, I headed back to the dorm and gave my mom a "homesick" call. My college experience already seemed doomed.

In desperation, I reached out to Abby, a high school friend attending a nearby college. And hey! She knew the Carolina Shag! I begged her for help. She came to visit me to give me some basics on the steps. Anyway, another case of someone empowering me—I could fit in a little better knowing this dance.

That came in handy during the fraternity rush, which back in 1979 happened at the very start of the school year. There were nonstop parties for a couple of weeks on what was known as Fraternity Row, a U-shaped street that housed six big frats. There, we mixed and mingled with the upperclassmen. After they sized us up, they ran a process called a *bid*. All of us would sit anxiously in our dorm rooms, waiting for that evening when there would be a knock on the door and one of us would get an envelope containing an invitation from one or more of the fraternities.

My roomies, all three of whom had been high school classmates, were all nervously awaiting that knock on the door. Me, I had only done the rush because I thought it was a great way to meet people and have some fun—but a fraternity was another aspect of college life I had to say no to. I knew I couldn't afford the dues. I also didn't drink, so maybe that would be a mark against me anyway.

But lo and behold, I received a bid from Kappa Alpha Order to join up. I felt honored and told the fraternity president so, but I also advised him I just couldn't pay for it. Here again, I was empowered. After the chapter leadership had an executive meeting, I was advised that I could have a "no dues" membership for the first year, which would allow me to be a completely active member. I was also elected pledge class president and initiated as a "brother" the following year. And at the end of that first year, I took my first drink … but not my last. (After all, I do own a winery … much more on that later).

I was also elected treasurer, because the treasurer never had to pay dues; it was part of the fraternity bylaws. Even though that role was usually filled by an upperclassman, they made an exception in my case. So despite my circumstances, they completely accepted me, and, as a result, I made some great lifetime friends. I remain a supporter of the chapter and the Kappa Alpha Order Educational Foundation to this day. Empowerment is a beautiful thing to pass on to the next guy.

Which was one of my first assignments as a freshman—because even though I wasn't going to play on the football team, I still ended up having to empower the team *off* the field. A lot of the kids (I say *kids*—but they were my age at the time!) had been recruited from rural schools. Since most of them hadn't done too well on their SATs, technically, they shouldn't have been accepted by the school. But the head football coach negotiated a deal with the dean of admissions— the school would create a study hall for the players whose test scores hadn't been up to snuff, and that study hall would be run by someone who could help them survive the academic demands of the college.

Guess who that someone was?

Even though I had only been going to Presbyterian College for about a month, I was already pretty familiar with the football coaching staff from when I was still thinking about joining the team.

> Even though I wasn't going to play on the football team, I still ended up having to empower the team off the field.

All the players were acquainted with me as well, because I worked out in the gym when they were around—they knew I had played in high school and I had been the captain, so they kind of accepted me as one of them. Since my test scores were high, the powers that be thought I had the perfect blend of skills to run that study hall. And since the school was going to pay me to do this, it was fine with me.

So there I was, with ten kids the same age as me in the study hall. A lot of them were in some of the same classes I was in, so it was easy for us to go through our homework assignments together and tackle whatever they were struggling with. I soon discovered they all obviously had a great work ethic. They wouldn't have been recruited if they hadn't put everything into being successful athletically. However, they had never really been challenged *academically*. They were excited to be in college—but intimidated by the fact that they were expected to actually pass their classes. They had to maintain a 2.0 GPA, or they'd be kicked off the team.

The biggest shock came when I realized many of them had no idea how to add fractions. If I asked them to add one-third to one-half, they had no idea that all you had to do was get a common denominator, change the one-half to three-sixths and the one-third to two-sixths, and add them together to get five-sixths. This was science fiction to some of them, and I instantly knew this task was not going to be an easy one.

I ended up batting .500 with my new students, to mix sports metaphors. About half of them made it on to graduate from college while surviving the demands of college sports. I like to think I made a difference in getting them through school and helping the football team hang on to some great players. I wish it would have worked for all of them, but I did all that I could.

A Momentous Meeting

At the start of my sophomore year, I wasn't dating anyone—my high school relationship had just ended that past summer. Remember my buddy Tim Wilson, the guy who became a comedian? Well, since he hadn't changed my life in a few years, he was due, and darned if he didn't deliver. At the time, he was dating a woman named Mary Perry, and one day he said to me out of the blue, "This suite mate of Mary's is either the nicest girl I've ever met—or she's a floozy. I'm not sure which."

That was quite a spectrum.

Anyway, he told me I needed to meet her. Her name was Lori, and she was a freshman. Well, I had just had the surgery done on my wrist that I talked about in the last chapter, so my right arm was in a cast. Ever try taking notes in class with your left hand when you're right handed? It wasn't easy—I'm not just talking about the actual writing; I'm also referring to my attempts to decipher my left-handed scrawl after the fact. But, what the heck: I approached her at the lunchroom and introduced myself, cast and all, explaining that Tim said I should meet her. Well, maybe Tim should have asked this girl a few questions in advance, because it turned out she already had a boyfriend lingering from high school, just like I did when I started college. So I was immediately shot down.

Cut to a week later.

It's a Thursday night. Tim's on the phone with Mary, trying to get her to go with him to the one pub in town that had music and pool tables—a great place to hang out. Mary was reluctant, I gathered, from Tim's side of the conversation. I don't know what got into me, but I said that if Mary brought Lori, then I'd go too. All four of us could go together. Tim relayed that message to Mary, and, to my surprise, the girls agreed. That was a win, a big win, bigger than I thought it was going to be in the long term.

We ended up having a great time that night, a whole lot of laughter and carrying on, with one story leading to another. I learned some interesting things about Lori—such as the fact that the dentist she'd had while growing up accidentally pulled a couple of her real teeth instead of her baby teeth and, as a result, she had to wear a retainer with two false teeth. She pulled it out to show me. I couldn't believe somebody would do that the first time we really hung out. But it didn't matter. We danced (the Carolina Shag, of course!), shot pool, and had a lot of fun.

Afterward, we walked back to the dorm, which had been built in a traditional southern style with the big columns out front. Since we weren't allowed in the girls' dorm back in those days, Tim and I both took our respective girls over to separate columns. To me, it had been a great date, and I was determined to get a good night kiss. Later, I discovered Lori was determined *not* to give me that kiss. But I got it. And as I walked back to the parking lot with Tim to get the car, he asked me what I thought. My answer?

"I bet you I will marry that girl."

I never dated anybody else. We got engaged in the spring of our senior year and were married a few months after graduation. I must have married an angel, because I can barely put up with myself—she's made it through forty years of being married to me! I was successful at the art of "marrying up"—definitely a big way to be empowered.

Double the Classes, Double the Fun

Making it to graduation ended up being a lot harder than I thought. I was doing great academically. I had only made one B my entire time there, and that was because I was talked into taking an honors English class—that subject was not my forte. As a senior, I was president of the Blue Key Honor Society; I was the number one student in the business school and in the top five of the whole school. I was about to successfully complete dual majors as well in my four years there, one in mathematics and one in business administration.

I was also one class shy of getting a minor in information technology, and I thought, why not go for it? Unfortunately, that IT class was only offered at the same time as the corporate finance class, one of the tougher ones in the business school. Not so tough for me, because, luckily, I had my mad math skills. The big problem was I couldn't be in two places at one time.

So I met with the corporate finance professor as well as the IT professor and gave them the same pitch: "If I can get permission from the dean, can I take both of your classes at the same time, as long as I show up for all tests and get all the assignments done?" They thought about it and gave me the green light.

When I met with the dean about this matter, he didn't quite know what to do at first. He said, "Well, we've never approved this for anybody before." However, he couldn't really think of a reason I shouldn't be allowed to do it, so … once again, green light.

How did I choose which of the two classes to attend? I didn't. I couldn't decide which one I should go to, so I seldom went to either one! Luckily, Lori coincidentally was taking the IT class, so she shared her notes with me. Because of my math major, I was qualified to tutor students in the finance class—and through them, I was also able to soak up the content.

The result? I managed to score As in *both* classes. But that wouldn't have happened if both my professors and the dean hadn't agreed to let me do it—and if my future wife hadn't agreed to share her notes!

———

During my college years, at every turn, whenever I ran into an obstacle, someone was there to help me get past it. And, of course, Tim was there to introduce me to the love of my life. I was proud of my record at Presbyterian College and, later on, even prouder to achieve my MBA from Clemson University. Higher education profoundly changed my life, and not just from what I learned in the classes. I made friends for life and met the mother of my children.

College certainly ended up being worth a lot more than the money and effort I put into it—even more than the academics I absorbed. It provided more fertile soil for this mustard seed to blossom. Now … it was time to enter the workplace.

CHAPTER 4

Empowered by

WORK

Maya Angelou once said, "Nothing will work unless you do."
I was totally unaware of that quote when I was first making my way in the world, but I sure as heck lived by that precept. From the moment when I got my first job as a dishwasher at that pizza parlor and developed my stool-jumping skills, I quickly learned that if I put everything I had into a task, I would succeed at it the majority of the time—and my effort would also be appreciated.

I sometimes envy people who have a calling. At an early age, they're passionate about what they want to be—whether it's a doctor, a writer, a teacher, a painter, a scientist, whatever. I only had one raging ambition when I graduated from high school—and that was to become an astronaut. My plan was to go to Georgia Tech, get an engineering degree, and build on my mathematics to pick up the kind of skill set NASA would be looking for. Unfortunately, this was right about the time that government funding for NASA began to dry up. I heard rumors that engineers there were being laid off left and right and some of them were driving taxis just to make the rent. If being an astronaut was my calling, well, then I would have to call it off. It wasn't going to happen.

So when I graduated from college, I had only one ambition—get a job.

To do that, I created the best, most professional résumé I could manage. Apparently I succeeded, because the college ended up using it as an example in their résumé class for seniors for years to come. And yet, even after I had attended all the job fairs available and interviewed with as many companies as possible, I ended up with only two job offers. One was as an entry-level finance person at Wells Fargo for $13,500 a year. The other was from a textile company, Milliken, which had sixty-five operating locations in North America alone. They were very aggressive in their recruiting and had a very high bar for making the cut. I was fortunate enough to get across that bar. They offered more—$17,500—and after six months on the job, they would also sponsor me getting my master's degree, which I could earn in night school classes. That excited me, because I knew that's the only way I could have afforded a higher degree.

> So I went into the textile business, even though all I knew about it was that textiles had something to do with the shirts I wore.

So I went into the textile business, even though all I knew about it was that textiles had something to do with the shirts I wore, a shirt you put on. But I finished at the top of the class and all that kind of stuff.

So I started my career in manufacturing at their location in Travelers Rest, North Carolina, near Greenville, South Carolina, an area with a population of about one hundred thousand. At the same time, my wife started a teaching job there—and, when I began going to night school for my MBA, she began going to night school for her EdM in gifted education.

The Horse Race

Milliken had about thirty thousand people working for them at the time, so it was easy to get lost in the shuffle, especially if you didn't deliver. I once attended a high-end function for our customers, and one of the company owners was there. I heard him remark to someone else, "My human resource strategy is to hire the very, very best out of college and ride them like stallions. Ride them until they wear out."

Many people would have been disturbed to hear this, but I wasn't. Instead, it made me feel better, because it was confirmation that the stress they put us all under was for a reason. It fired me up, because I wasn't going to get worn out; I was going to stay in this horse race, and I was going to cross the finish line.

The competition was fierce, however. Milliken hired about four hundred college grads a year, and all of us had to have had a 3.85 GPA or better. They would first put you to work in a plant for about six months, then send you to corporate headquarters for leadership development with forty or fifty others who had also been hired right out of college. There was a lot to learn in that program—there were plant tours, tech workshops, lessons on statistical process control, and so forth. It was a demanding process, and I estimate that, five years in, there were only forty of us left from that initial pool of four hundred. But I survived and even thrived because I put in the work.

Eventually, I was promoted to department manager of the finishing plant, one of three divisions of this particular manufacturing facility. The other two divisions were the knitting plant, where Larry Blood was the department manager, and the dye house, where

Mike Hargett was the department manager. Larry, Mike, and I were all about the same age, maybe a year or two apart, and we were all committed to completing the Milliken "horse race."

It was intense. The company was very big on metrics, so our departments' stats on quality, efficiency, and on-time delivery were very, very visible to all. The competition between the three of us to do the best job soon became very heated. Yet, in spite of that, we also became lifetime friends. We respected each other but weren't afraid to mix it up when someone came looking to point fingers. If there was some kind of quality problem, Larry might say, "The dye house messed up", Mike might say, "The finishing department dropped the ball", and I might say, "It's a knitting problem!"

I thrived on the competition—I loved it! We each pursued the best performance in quality, efficiency, safety, productivity, retention, engagement, and more. We would even compete over who had the best housekeeping in the plant. We were also competitive "off the field," as our standing Saturday morning golf game was filled with handicap debates, bets, and side bets.

We all believed in the empowerment of work, and our rivalry drove the three of us forward to achieve more than we might have otherwise. As a result, we became known as "The Three Horsemen." And we became friends for life. I fish with Mike every other year, and his kids know my kids. Larry lives only an hour away. Both of them have also either worked for me or with me at a few other companies during our professional journeys. Yes, these young stallions are now old warhorses—but we're still able to run pretty good when we get the chance.

Competition doesn't have to be a bad thing. It can force you to sharpen your skills, improve your mental edge, and max out your motivation. By competing with integrity, we empowered each other to be the best we could be. We continually raised the bar for each other. And we were all proud of the results of that effort.

I also formed a special bond with my boss, Tony Raffo, a mountain of a man standing tall at six foot five and weighing in at around three hundred pounds. He came from the human resources side of the business and then worked his way into general leadership and general management. Everything about him was larger than life, including the stories he told, and people really respected him. He was the kind of guy who, if he were a military commander, would tell the troops to go climb a mountain and they'd climb it, no questions asked. That worked at Milliken because he had the numbers to back him up. At his next company, that wouldn't be the case, and I would be stuck in the foxhole with him when we had angry customers on our backs 24-7. More on that in the next chapter.

Overall, Milliken was a great place to start my career. I was there for ten years and ended up in ten different positions by climbing the company ladder. I was swing shift manager, then department manager, superintendent and quality manager, pursuit of excellence director, plant manager, and finally business manager. I also learned many of the business leadership skills that would serve me well in the years to come. The way the company developed its employees really paid off for me.

And I also learned something very valuable about myself in the process, but it wasn't easy to take on board. Let me tell you about that next.

Looking in the Mirror

You know the old saying "All work and no play makes Jack a dull boy?" Earlier in this chapter, I mentioned I discovered something of a downside to my relentless work ethic. If you want a clue to what that was all about, just call me *Jack*. Here's what happened.

After I had been promoted at Milliken a couple of times, I was told by one of my supervisors that he wanted me to enter a leadership development program. All of us were required to get forty hours of outside training a year anyway, so it sounded like this would be a great way to accomplish that. I went to Denver for the class, which was run by clinical psychologists and included "students" who were actually high-powered business leaders from all sorts of industries.

The first thing all of us had to do for this class was take a personality test. Not only that, but we also had to go to the people we worked with and ask *them* to complete an assessment of us. I was given a certain number of packets to distribute for that purpose. I wouldn't know who had said what, so they were free to be as honest about me as possible. In other words, I was about to experience the clash between how I perceived myself and how others perceived me. At the start, I wasn't too worried about my results, but then I saw several people, including executive vice presidents and the like, driven to tears by the discrepancy between their private and public selves. Maybe that's when I got a little nervous about what I would find out about me.

> We come at experiences from different backgrounds and different perspectives and have different ways of interpreting them.

It turned out to be one of the most eye-opening moments of my life, and one that has stuck with me since.

I had considered myself to be very personable up until I took that class. I seemed to get along with everyone pretty well and did everything I could to develop strong bonds at work. Naturally, I thought people regarded me as a nice, friendly guy.

Well, that's when it was really driven home to me that we come at experiences from different backgrounds and different perspectives and have different ways of interpreting them. The way I see something may not be the same way you see it. If you've read this far in the book, you already know I'm a guy who's committed to getting a job done. That's my mental priority and my primary focus. My feedback reflected that—it indicated people seemed to consider me to be smart, driven, and committed—all great qualities, right?

What wasn't so great was people did not consider me to be a *caring person*. That was because when I would show up at the plant, I would immediately switch into work mode. I wouldn't take the time to ask someone about their weekend, their family, what was going on with them, all that kind of stuff, because when I was on the job, small talk was not on my mind at all. I immediately made every conversation about work. To others at the plant, that indicated a lack of interest in them and their lives.

Upon reflection, I realized it was more about my mindset of getting things done than anything else. From an early age, I always had work to do and not a lot of time to do it. Over the years, that caused me to build up some pretty big emotional blinders that prevented me from really engaging with people on a deeper level—simply because it took time away from my tasks.

Clearly, now that I was an adult in leadership roles, I had to make an effort to change that behavior. My wife, Lori, helped me with that effort. We would come home from a social event and she would evaluate me on my interactions. Did I talk too much, or did I let everyone else share their stories? When others were talking, was I a good listener? Did I show interest? Lori was an excellent coach and helped empower me to modify how I related to others.

Flash forward to today. I now feel I'm pretty disciplined when it comes to talking to everyone from new acquaintances to old friends. I observe the 80/20 rule, which means I try to listen 80 percent of the time and talk 20 percent of the time. And when I do talk, I try to make sure that whatever I'm talking about is relevant to that person. It's helped me be a better leader, because I now have improved engagement with clients, staff, and everyone else around me at work.

Yes, work has empowered me greatly. Yes, you have to do your job well. But you should never forget your humanity in the process. That is *not* a good look for a servant leader!

CHAPTER 5

Empowered by
PERSEVERANCE

Working at Milliken was a real growth experience. I was able to climb the corporate ladder pretty quickly over the nine years I spent there, as well as learn the textile business from the ground up. I felt empowered there. People respected me and depended on me, and I did everything in my power to deliver—correction, *over*deliver—on what was expected of me.

I had lots of resources at my disposal at Milliken. That made getting things done a lot easier than they would have been otherwise. I was about to find out how to cope without those kinds of support systems—and be tested as I had never been before professionally.

I learned a few lessons during a very difficult time at my new employer's plant—and those lessons empowered me in very different ways. How do you handle constant stress when you're stuck in a situation you are completely helpless to resolve? I was about to find out.

Moving On from Milliken

Roger Milliken—you remember him, he's the one who referred to the new employees as "stallions"—was getting up there in age. He realized he needed a leadership succession plan and hired a guy named Tom Malone to be president of the company. That meant all the division presidents would be reporting to him.

One of those division presidents was Tony Raffo, the three-hundred-pound Italian whom I had bonded with. Well, Tony didn't get along too well with Tom and felt, long term, the personality clash wasn't going to improve any. So he decided to look outside the company for a new gig.

He found it at Chatham.

Chatham was a textiles manufacturer that had opened its doors all the way back in 1877. The company had been family owned—but the two Chatham men who ran it both unexpectedly passed away in their early sixties. Their children didn't want to run the business, so Tony was able to connect them with CMI Industries, a private equity holding company. CMI bought Chatham, and it became one of three textile operations they owned, along with Clinton Mills (the *CM* in CMI) in Clinton, South Carolina, and Elastic Fabrics of America in Greensboro, North Carolina. Tony became the CEO of Chatham.

Tony recruited three senior people from Milliken to make the change with him, with me included in that trio. He put me in charge of the furniture fabric division, which was located in a very large complex of plants, all on East Main Street in Elkin, North Carolina. Chatham was Elkin's number one employer—which wasn't hard, because Elkin was a very small town, so small we didn't think we'd like living there. We had been living in Greenville, South Carolina, which had a population of around one hundred thousand—Elkin, in contrast, had only six thousand people in its city limits. At first, the solution seemed simple. I said to my wife, Lori, "Well, we'll just live in Winston-Salem, which is comparable in size, and I'll just commute forty-five minutes to work."

But before we could go to Winston-Salem to explore our living options, I thought maybe we should stop by Elkin first just to see what the town was all about. I knew a few people there already and set Lori up to meet them. We both got the sense of it being a very, very warm and inviting town, kind of like a Mayberry for the '90s, and we fell in love with it. We never moved on to look at Winston-Salem. And luckily, since Lori was a teacher, she could pretty much work anywhere and easily found a new job. I have to take my hat off to this woman: my career took me to a lot of places we never expected to live—but Lori was always game and supportive. I'm a lucky man to have her. She did in fact empower me to go where I needed to go in order to be successful and always adapted well—even in China! More on that later …

Culture Clash

Chatham was not only located in a smaller town, but it was also a much smaller operation than Milliken. The family hadn't really been aggressive in expanding Chatham the way the Millikens had been with their company. They also hadn't been too interested in keeping up with the times in terms of work culture. In some ways, it still felt like they were in the nineteenth century!

Back at Milliken, Roger, the owner—who was worth about $2 billion—did not have his own designated parking space. He, like every other employee, simply parked wherever there was an empty space. That was his way, and I admired it. He didn't want to be differentiated from the other employees. There was no executive dining room or any of that kind of elitism.

At Chatham, however, if you were at any management level beyond frontline supervision, you had a parking spot with your name and title on it. Those in the highest positions had parking spaces closest to the front door. There was also an executive dining room so the bigwigs wouldn't have to eat with the hoi polloi. I was already a firm believer in servant leadership, but Chatham was structured more as a traditional top-to-bottom hierarchy.

And then there was what I called our "Vietnam War"—a terrible safety process that was literally hurting our people every day. Someone's finger would get cut, another would end up pulling a muscle—there was just an endless parade of injuries, some major and some minor, that I had never experienced before at Milliken. When we began to change the safety policy and require that all injuries be reported when they happened, we were stunned at how many people were being hurt. Nobody had bothered to keep track before!

> We were stunned at how many people were being hurt. Nobody had bothered to keep track before!

Tony quickly saw what had to be done. We did a lot of basics in terms of eliminating the exccutive dining room, eliminating the private parking, and putting in place safety training and ethics training. After I had been there for a few months, Tony realized that there wasn't even any kind of sexual harassment policy or training in place. We were amazed, because we had just come from a company where all that was just standard operating procedure. So what we did was put up signs in all the plants as a temporary Band-Aid, to let everyone know sexual harassment wasn't going to be tolerated.

After that, it didn't take long for the first shoe to drop.

It was a couple of weeks after we put up the signage. Early in the morning, Mavis, who was a weaver in one of our plants, came to the front office to talk to Tony, because he had an open-door policy in terms of seeing employees. After Tony's assistant, Joyce, told Mavis he was available, he saw her out his door and called out to her. "Mavis, come on in. What's on your mind?"

My office was adjacent to his, so I could hear every word of their conversation. She began by saying, "Mr. Raffo, I think I may be a victim of sexual harassment." Tony asked her to explain. "Well, as you know," she began, "weave plant two has three machine rows. Row A is the oldest, row B is second oldest, and row C has our newest machines. Since we're paid an incentive piece rate schedule, the more picks my machines throw, the more money I make."

I heard Tony say, "Go on."

"Bobby Joe is my third shift manager," she continued. "As you can see, I am fairly well endowed. Bobby Joe told me that if he can grab a feel off me at the start of a shift, he will assign me to row C, where I can get the most done. But if I'm not in the mood for his childlike country-boy behavior, he puts me on row A, where I will get the least done. Is that considered sexual harassment like on the signs you guys just posted?"

I wasn't in the room with them, but I wouldn't doubt Tony looked like he was about to have a heart attack.

"JOYCE!" he yelled out to his assistant. "Get Gary up here ASAP!" Gary was our HR manager. Gary came up, escorted Mavis to his office, and took her statement; then he sent her home. After that, he called Bobby Joe up to his office after his shift was done. Bobby Joe quickly verified Mavis's claim. But he blamed it on the old operations president who had told everyone they had one free pass on this kind of thing, but if they did it again, they would get fired. So Bobby Joe thought it would settle matters if he promised not to do it anymore.

Gary told him, "Dude, it doesn't work that way. You're fired." I walked him out the door. He was gone. And from that point on, the culture changed permanently. People suddenly knew there were rules about that sort of thing, and they had to abide by them.

However, there is an interesting postscript to this story, which demonstrates the dangers of having a big business in a very small town. Later on, Mavis went back to Gary, and she was really mad. Not because of what happened to her, but because of what happened to Bobby Joe!

"I didn't want you to fire him. Hell, he lives two blocks from me, and his cousin is married to my uncle's nephew. I just wanted him to stop!"

Sometimes you just can't win, but these were the kinds of situations that can happen when you employ six thousand people, the same number of people who lived in the town. Personal and professional interests will clash!

But what came out of the whole thing was very significant. We were able to move this hundred-year-old company into the 1990s in terms of management style, behavior, ethics, and safety. But change like that never comes without some pain. Some people missed what they considered "the good old days" and how things were done in the past. But I believe the new culture we put in place empowered everyone to feel safe, secure, and respected on the job, and that was a whole lot more important than a few people here and there who weren't in the mood for progress.

Under Pressure

During this initial period at Chatham, business went through the roof. That was good for the bottom line but not so good for me. I just didn't have the manufacturing capacity to get all the orders out the door. Chatham's other two businesses were automotive and blankets, and, on paper anyway, they were more profitable than the one I was running. However, my business unit ran the vertical yarn manufacturing operations that were the foundation of the complex (the other two units purchased the yarn for weaving). Regardless, Tony was putting the bulk of the weaving resources into them—mostly into the automotive business, because we were one of only five domestic suppliers of fabric to the carmakers. I was low man on the totem pole.

The year 1994 turned out to be one of the most stressful years of my professional life. No matter how hard I worked, no matter how hard my people worked, we just could never catch up with our backlog of orders, simply because we didn't have the resources to manufacture at the scale we needed to at the time.

In short, it was a brutal time. My phone was filled with nothing but angry people all day long. I'm a guy who likes to get the job done—and, for the first time in my life, there was no way to get the job done. It was a lot of tension to manage, and I had never gone through anything like it. I would actually drive down the interstate every once in a while to let loose some tears on my own, so nobody else would see just how upset about this situation I was.

As I said, smaller clients had to cope with the longest wait times. And, at the time, one of those clients was a church. We were the largest producer of tufted church pew fabric in North America, but because that business was so fragmented, those clients were placed very low on my priority list.

It was in the middle of this crisis that a preacher called me up.

Even though all I was getting on the phone were complaints, I still answered each and every call. I felt it was my duty to be as transparent as possible with these people who were justifiably irritated. So I took the preacher's call. He was from Kentucky and explained how his new church was opening soon and the only holdup was—you guessed it—the fabric for the pews. The manufacturer had told him the delay was due to the fabric not arriving. And I represented the fabric supplier.

I tried logic. I explained our capacity challenges, customer prioritization, all the normal protocols for this kind of situation. He did not want to hear about any of that. His voice got louder and louder as he talked about how the church committee had spent hours on the design, color, and fabric selection for their new house of worship. I had nothing to offer except more excuses. That's when I heard his fist hit the desk in his office, as he proclaimed, "You are preventing souls from being saved by Christ! You are the one standing in the way of my church opening!"

I had already been called many things in my career, but never had I been accused of being an instrument of the devil. Being a church-going man, that left me feeling a wee bit disturbed …

Finally, I asked him for the address of the church and the date he was planning to open it up. He told me. And then I committed to having nice padded folding chairs delivered to the church, enough to seat the whole congregation and then some. That would get him by until we could deliver the fabric to the manufacturer.

He was quiet a moment. I could almost feel what he was thinking. He had his heart set on getting that fabric, but he also had it set on opening the church when he had planned to. This was not his ideal solution, but it *was* a solution. He thanked me, even though it was clear he was not happy about it. But I was relieved. I would no longer be the one standing between souls and Jesus!

Anyway, I picked up the chairs from a rental place and delivered them to the church in time. And a few months later, when the actual church pew fabric finally did arrive, the chairs were picked up by the rental company and returned to storage. A happy ending? Happy, yes, but an ending? Not yet!

A few years later, some old friends of ours in South Carolina called. They asked me, "Is this the same Derrill that gives chairs to churches in Kentucky so they can open on time?"

That was a question designed to confuse, especially, as I've said, as I was the only Derrill in the world as far as I knew. Bewildered, I asked how they knew about what had happened between me and the preacher. The answer shocked me. The preacher was now traveling from town to town as an evangelist—and, when he performed his sermons, he would tell three stories about overcoming adversity. One of them was about being empowered to triumph over difficulties. It was about me and the chairs. In his telling, I had given him more than a solution—I had made him realize that he did not need a completely perfect church to spread the Word. He just needed a place for people to gather and hear his message. He felt as though I had empowered him to see and accept other solutions when the best one was unavailable. To quote him, "Derrill helped me open my mind and spirit to other possibilities."

I guess you could say he was spreading the word about empowerment through my actions! And after I heard all that, I guessed maybe Saint Peter might open the gate for me after all when the time came to meet up.

But my stressful circumstances continued. A flood of angry calls still awaited me every day in my office as we fell further and further behind. Trade magazines alerted their readers that it was taking us six months to fulfill orders, which was unheard of in this industry. My integrity was taking hits right and left, and it took its toll on me.

One day, while I was handling yet another furious customer, Tony wandered into my office and watched as I finished up the call and hung up. Sensing my mental state (which wasn't hard), he asked, "Rice, you're not having a very good day, are you?" I shot him a look that said, without saying it, "Are you freakin' kidding me?" That's when he said one simple sentence that completely altered my perspective.

"Rice, remember, we're not saving lives, we're not rescuing children … *it's just polyester*."

I blinked in confusion, and then he said, "Let's go get a haircut." My blood pressure shot up again. "A haircut? Now? No way, I got a million phone calls to return!" He shook his head. "No. We're going to get haircuts."

And we did.

In that moment, Tony grounded me. He made me realize that, no, we weren't saving the world at the plant. This was just a job; we were just manufacturing fabric, and I was doing the best possible job under the circumstances. There was no reason to make it about me or take the customer abuse too personally. The situation was to blame, not me. That empowered me to take a little of that emotional load off my shoulders.

———————

Tony ended up leaving the company because, even though revenue was higher than it ever had been, profitability was low. I became the senior executive in his stead. Once I became president, I was very visible. I'd come in at night and walk through the plants and say hello to people. And when I did town hall meetings, we worked it out so we'd shut down the plants so everybody could come. This was the first time I was able to put my own brand of servant leadership to work on a company-wide basis, and the results

> Once I became president, I was very visible.

were worth all the pain I had endured. I felt like I had been through hell and back—but I didn't abandon ship, and now I was the captain of it! That's what I call *empowerment*—persevering even when the going gets tough and actually finding a rainbow after the storm blows over. Suddenly, I was really enjoying my time at Chatham.

And in the town of Elkin as well. When you're the president of the company that basically supports the entire town, people regard you as sort of a junior mayor. So I suddenly found myself getting involved in almost everything going on there. They put me on the hospital board and the Chamber of Commerce, and I was named president of an arts council. I wouldn't have had all those positive experiences if I hadn't stuck it out at Chatham. As Kenny Rogers once sang, "You got to know when to hold 'em, know what to fold 'em." I'm glad I held 'em.

In Elkin, you truly couldn't go anywhere where somebody didn't know you. That didn't feel oppressive to us, however, because it was such a nice friendly town, the kind of place where you could literally knock on someone's door and ask if you could borrow a cup of sugar. Kids could also ride their bikes up and down the street without their parents having to worry about them. The longer we lived there, the more it felt like Mayberry. And that's why we've always kept our home there, despite our many travels over the years.

Speaking of travels, you're about to hear about our most radical move in chapter 7. You want to get out of your comfort zone bigtime? Move your family to China!

But first, we'll take a little inspiration break …

CHAPTER 6

Empowered by

INSPIRATION

W e are all inspired by the great accomplishments of seemingly
ordinary people, and I'm no exception. That's why I wanted
to use this chapter not only as a break from my own empowerment
stories but also to focus on some great people who not only overcame
obstacles but crushed them in the process.

There are all sorts of amazing geniuses, champions, and leaders
who are now household names—but there was a time when nobody
knew them from Adam. They, too, had their struggles in finding
their way by encountering humiliating setbacks that probably made
many people around them wonder why they didn't just throw up
their hands and give up. Undoubtedly, there were (and still are) others
with their level of skills, talents, and intellects—but these are people
who perhaps never lived up to their potential because they bowed to
negative circumstances instead of challenging them.

These legends didn't.

Abraham Lincoln. Routinely considered our greatest president ever by historians and the public alike. Well, before he ascended to that highest position in our land, he had been soundly defeated *eight times* in other elections.

Michael Jordan. Routinely called the greatest basketball player ever. And yet, he was cut from his high school's varsity team and demoted to junior varsity.

Albert Einstein. His name is shorthand for *genius*. Well, at first, nobody thought he was anything of the kind. He did not speak until he was three. And later, while at school in Munich, his teacher reported that "nothing good would ever come of the young Einstein."

Wait, as the commercials say, there's more!

Pelé, perhaps the greatest soccer player ever, grew up in poverty. He could not afford a proper soccer ball and usually played with either a grapefruit or a sock stuffed with newspaper and tied with a string. **Sachin Tendulkar**, known as the "God of Cricket," served as a mere ball boy in the 1987 Cricket World Cup and became one of the sport's best batsmen. While here in the US, a Black man named Cassius Clay triumphed over a white-dominated society by becoming the heavyweight boxing champion, changing his name to **Muhammad Ali** and becoming a vital political and social force.

And there's *still* more!

The creator of the fantastically successful Harry Potter series, **J. K. Rowling**, had her first Potter book rejected by twelve publishers before one bought the manuscript. **Walt Disney** was fired from an early job at the *Kansas City Star* newspaper—because they said he wasn't creative enough! **Elvis Presley** drove a truck before he wandered into Sun Studios to record a song for his mother's birthday—and the rest is music history.

The list does indeed go on and on. **Stephen Hawking**, a man who couldn't move, traveled to space. **Mahatma Gandhi**, an Indian lawyer with a very basic education, went on to lead his nation in a successful nonviolent uprising against England's rule. **Oprah Winfrey** survived an abusive and impoverished childhood to become an international television mogul.

All these icons believed they could be more than anyone else thought they were capable of. And they fulfilled the promise that was inside them. May we all be able to achieve the same!

Alan

That brings me to my younger brother, Alan. He too had to overcome an incredible roadblock that was placed directly in his path—me.

As he would put it to me, "You're a hard act to follow." I don't mean to come off as egotistical here, but the fact is I had an outstanding record through high school and college, in academics and athletics, and then built a successful career in textiles. He followed my exact same trajectory in the exact same schools (and even the same business after college), and was constantly billed as "Derrill's younger brother." Which could be a good thing or a bad thing, as I'm about to explain.

> These icons believed they could be more than anyone else thought they were capable of. And they fulfilled the promise that was inside them.

But first, let me cop to some of the harassment I engaged in—as most older siblings do with their younger ones.

For example, there was a time that there were no Crunch Berries in Cap'n Crunch cereal. For you younger readers, I know that seems unimaginable, but yes, they invented those little purple orbs of sugar during our childhood, and Alan *loved* him some. Well, one Saturday morning, I got up before he did, went into the kitchen, took out that box of Cap'n Crunch with Crunch Berries, and meticulously removed every single Crunch Berry from that box, one at a time. I put the "berries" in a separate food container, hid the container, and then put the box of cereal back where it was. Then I went into the other room to watch TV. Soon enough, I heard Alan enter the kitchen and make himself a bowl of cereal ... and I waited for the explosion. I didn't have to wait long.

"MOM! DERRILL STOLE THE CRUNCH BERRIES!"

Okay, I got in a little trouble for that one, and I'm not sure what I was thinking when I did it. I just thought it was funny as all get-out.

We also used to play blindman's bluff, where a bunch of us would turn off all the lights. One of us would be blindfolded and was expected to feel around in the dark to try to find the rest of us. If the person touched you, you were out of the game.

Well, I had a little trick where, in a corner in the hallway, I could put my feet on the wall behind me, place my hands on the walls on either side of me (I was a Spider-Man in training) and climb up to the ceiling. That drove Alan crazy, because he was still short enough that he would walk under me and never know I was hovering there above his head. I would make some noises just to tease him, but he just couldn't find me!

That's normal kids' horseplay, but there was a serious undertow to our sibling rivalry. Alan, unfortunately, was not as strong in the academic arena as I was. My mom therefore downplayed my school successes at home because she always worried about Alan feeling bad about them. But he had a similar strength in sports. Alan was three years younger than me. In high school, when I was a senior on the varsity football team, he was a freshman on the junior varsity team. At the sports banquet that year, we both got all the same athletic awards for our teams—we were both the defensive captains—he just didn't get the academic award.

Then he went to the same college as me. Again, when I was a senior, he was just a freshman. At the time, I was a fraternity officer, president of the Blue Key society, the number one student in the business school, and number two in the school overall. So, again, he must have felt a lot of pressure to live up to my image.

That started from day one. During the fraternity rush that fall, being Derrill's little brother got him into a bit of trouble. As I noted back in chapter 3, there was Fraternity Row, the U-shaped street that housed six big frats. Alan goes to the first fraternity on the block, and they get excited, because "Hey, guys, look, it's Derrill's little brother!"

This was, of course, an excuse to get him stinking drunk. They made him do a beer bong, where you basically had a whole can of beer poured into your mouth through a tube. Alan had never done one of these before, but after the first one, he was still pretty solid. But then he went to the next one, and the next one … and each time, it was, "Oh, it's Derrill Rice's little brother! Give him a beer bong!"

By the time he made it to the fourth house, he was pretty hammered—which he realized when he ran out to the back deck and threw up in the yard. That made him decide that maybe it was time for him to just quietly leave and walk home, without making a big deal about it.

Between the fraternities and the dorms was about five hundred yards of football field, three practice fields all in all. And in the middle of that set of fields was a concrete house with basic bathrooms in them so players wouldn't have to go all the way back to the gymnasium to go during practice. Well, when Alan got to that building, he somehow got it in his mind that he was at his dorm. He opened the door, neatly folded his clothes, lay down on the floor, and went to sleep. The next morning, a little slice of sunshine came in through the bathroom window and woke him up. He opens the door, looks out, and sees it's daytime. And then he let forth with a loud expletive.

It was the first day of classes—and he had just missed his first one.

He ran out the door, then he realized he had no clothes on. He ran back in, grabbed his clothes, put them on, and hurried to his dorm room so he could brush his teeth. But it was already too late.

Anyway, Alan turned it all around, because he, like my wife, Lori, never met a stranger—he made friends with everyone. And it got to the point where it went from him being called Derrill Rice's little brother to me being called Alan Rice's big brother!

When he graduated, he too went to work for Milliken as I did—his first job was at a plant of theirs in Alma, Georgia. But he didn't stay with Milliken very long, and if you asked him now, he would tell you he should have. Milliken was very well run, but smaller companies gave him financial incentives to leave, which seemed great in the moment. However, when he went to work for them, he quickly saw they weren't up to par. And once you left Milliken, you didn't get back in. So he had some difficult career adjustments to make, especially when the textile business began to seriously decline in the area.

He and his wonderful wife, Wendy, both have great careers now. They raised two girls who are now out of college and also working hard toward their futures. And let me tell you one more fascinating fact about Alan—and this is something I do not say lightly. But the man is the best air guitar player in the world.

My brother and his family now also take care of our mom, who, as I write this, is eighty-six. I moved her into a house in Elkin near our home years ago, but because my career has had me on the move so much, we all agreed it would be better to move to Alan's town in Georgia, where not only he and his wife but also their daughters live. She's only a few miles from Alan, and he regularly stops over to check on her and take care of the garbage and other stuff like that.

So my hat's off to Alan for surviving me, surviving a morning without Crunch Berries, surviving multiple beer bongs, and going on to make an impressive life for himself. We only see each other a couple of times a year, but when we do, it's very useful. After all, we share the same genetics, so when we compare our aches and pains as we get older, we frequently find we have the same issues. As a matter of fact, you could call me his early warning system, because I let him know just what's going to be hurting him, whether it's his hip, shoulder, or lower back, in a few years.

I have been empowered over the years by watching my brother overcome adversity and accomplish great things. He had a belief that the Lord would show him the way. His journey is truly inspiring to me.

CHAPTER 7

Empowered by
RISK

Change isn't always pretty. But if you go with the tide instead of against it, I believe you can always find your footing. The transition may be painful and difficult at times, but in the end, making a big move can enrich your life and take you in new productive paths that will energize your personal growth.

Big moves, however, require *risk*—particularly when you're heading into uncharted waters. You just don't know how the chance you're taking will pay off—but it makes more sense to do something rather than do nothing, especially when you know time is running out.

> I needed to be empowered by risk—or I soon would be a man without an industry.

That was where I was in 2009. I needed to be empowered by risk—or I soon would be a man without an industry.

Here's why. In 1994, the US textile industry hit a record profit. It continued to post strong numbers for four more years, despite increasing competition from cheaper foreign imports. Then in 1998, those numbers suddenly took a big hit. The currencies of many Asian countries had collapsed, causing goods shipped from those nations to suddenly get even cheaper. Over the next four years, Asian currencies fell by 40 percent while textile imports to America grew by 80 percent. In the year 2000, the textile industry as a whole posted its first annual loss ($700 million) in the more than fifty years that the statistic had been kept![4] In that same year, more than sixty thousand US textile jobs were lost.

My industry could no longer afford to be competitive. And there was a chance I could be left out in the cold professionally.

As I mentioned in chapter 5, the company I ran, Chatham, was one of three holdings by the private equity firm CMI. Another one of them, Clinton Mills, just couldn't stay afloat during this difficult time and went under. As they were going bankrupt, CMI decided it couldn't wait any longer to divest. Since Chatham was its most profitable company, they sold it first—to Interface, an Atlanta-based publicly traded company that had a textiles division.

Down the line, I ended up changing companies and took a job running the Burlington House division of the International Textile Group. I was recruited by Joe Gorga, who was the location manager at Milliken when I first began my job there out of college. Joe was blunt with me. "I'm not really sure what to do with this business," he said. "It's losing money, and you need to either shut it down or turn it around."

I was determined to turn it around. That's when it came to me— if you can't beat 'em, join 'em!

---

4   Eric Heisler, "Asian Meltdown Blamed for Textile Crisis," *The Greensboro News & Record*, updated January 25, 2015, https://greensboro.com/asian-meltdown-blamed-for-textile-crisis-cheap-labor-will-always-be-a-factor-but-some/article_64f94077-f61-571c-a0a2-dde0f1ec1cdf.html.

China or Bust!

One of my major strategies was to build a manufacturing footprint in Asia so that I would have the same cost basis for our materials. I had already developed a supply chain there, which necessitated my traveling back and forth, so I had gotten to know a bit about the region and thought I could pull it off. So I made a presentation to the board to build a plant in China and got the green light.

From there, I did my own direct negotiations with what the Chinese termed their *enterprise zones*, which were allowed to embrace more free market principles than the rest of the country to attract foreign investments such as ours. I oversaw the construction, setup, and hiring, and the end product was a plant in Jiaxing, which is still running today.

That did the trick. I turned the company around. And because of the experience I gained from that effort, I was asked to develop a newly acquired arm of the International Textile Group, Airbag Asia, which, as you might have guessed from the name, was going to be focused on airbag production for vehicles. Wilbur Ross, who went on to become the US Secretary of Commerce, owned the company and asked me to take on the role of president and create a business plan to build a plant for it in China.

This wasn't a job I could do long distance or by taking the occasional trip overseas. Nope, I had to actually be there to make it work. I told my family we were all going to have to relocate and held my breath for their reaction. Well, Lori was unbelievably supportive and was ready to put all her energies into the move. Our daughter, Caroline, was just about to start college at NYU, so she would have been gone most of the time anyway. It was a little more complicated with our son, Austin, who was about to be a freshman in high school. Lori, being the dedicated educator she was, searched for the best school for

Austin there and settled on the Shanghai American School. They had a pretty stringent admission policy, but Austin, who was excellent at academics, cleared the bar and was enrolled.

The next step was to find a place for all of us to live. I discovered a place called the Shanghai Racquet Club, which was an expat community that was walking distance from Austin's new school. On another one of my solo trips, I rented an apartment there, took a few photos of the place with my phone, and sent them home with the message "Here's where we're going to live." Then I lined up some rental furniture to be delivered there before we arrived as a family.

The next thing we had to deal with were the joys of an international move. For those of you who haven't done it, the big problem is you don't get most of your stuff for at least a month—your belongings get packed into a container and sent by ship. That's why I needed the rental furniture. Beyond that, we were only allowed to take eleven suitcases with us on the plane and their contents had to hold us over until then. Challenging, but doable. We made it all work, and we were ready to go.

And then … *kaboom*. Everything blew up in our faces.

It was the day before we would be flying to our new home. The container truck had just taken all the stuff that would be shipped. Everything was set. And then the phone rang. It was Joe, my boss. And he said five words I definitely did *not* want to hear—"We have a little problem."

The problem wasn't so little.

It was 2009. If you remember that time, you will certainly recall how our country's financial foundation was threatening to break apart at the seams. The Great Recession was suddenly in full swing, and one of its first victims was the automotive industry, where sales took an immediate nosedive. Well, if nobody's buying cars, nobody needs airbags. As a result, Wilbur Ross filed for Chapter 11 bankruptcy for the global airbag business unit, which naturally included Airbag Asia.

"Well, Joe," I replied after he filled me in on all this horrible news, "I'm supposed to be on a plane tomorrow with my family. We're all packed up and everything." I paused as I quickly worked things out in my head. "But we're still going," I said confidently. "I'll continue running my business in North America from China until we figure out how to handle this situation." I knew Wilbur Ross wanted to hold on to the airbag company; his intent was just to give all his creditors a haircut. Maybe he'd make it work.

It was worth the risk.

We flew out as scheduled the next morning, unsure of what would happen after the move. On the same flight, we were unaware that another family—Steve and Doreen Merkt and their two kids—was onboard and also relocating to China. They were also moving into the same complex as us. And for the capper, their son, Harrison, would be going to the same school as our Austin in Shanghai, while their daughter, Sam, was starting in a few weeks at NYU, the same college as our Caroline was about to attend! Crazy! But we didn't find out about all this until later. And by "we," I mean Lori!

That was a good omen, as opposed to what we found when we walked into our new apartment—it was completely empty! None of the rental furniture had been delivered as promised. I could see the look on Lori's face—she wasn't happy. Austin kept on his brave face, which I appreciated. I hustled to fix the situation and get us something to sit on (not to mention something to sleep on, eat at, etc.).

Two days later, things had improved to the point where Lori informed me we had a soccer game scheduled for that evening.

"Soccer game?" I asked.

By this time, she had met up with Steve and Doreen and found out all about them—including the fact that they were soccer players. That was whom we would be playing against.

It was on. Both my kids played and played well—after all, my daughter had even been captain of the soccer team in high school! We went out on this area covered with artificial turf and, as the sun set, we played soccer. And sadly, the Rice family was on the losing end of this match. I was definitely the weakest link. However, the outcome of the game didn't matter. What did matter was that was the beginning of a friendship that not only proved pivotal to our time in China but continues to this day.

My work schedule broke down this way: Mornings, I would focus on running the business back in America, and afternoons, I would pivot to creating a development plan for the building of the airbag plant. Meanwhile, my wife flew back with Caroline to help get her set up at NYU—we couldn't help but worry about our little girl being alone in the Big Apple with us being half a world away. Meanwhile, Austin had to adapt to being one of the few Caucasians in his school—and the only one of two on his baseball team. Most of the other kids were either from Japan, Korea, or Hong Kong.

I had my own huge challenge to face—the fact that I had moved my family to China to work for a company that was filing for bankruptcy. Wilbur Ross's gamble unfortunately did not pay off, and neither did mine—the creditors took the company from Wilbur Ross, and my mission was suddenly terminated. That's the downside of risk. Things can go sideways pretty quickly. But that's also what makes it exciting.

We thought we should at least let Austin finish his first year in high school before making another big move. And, in the meantime, I took my new free time and used it to look around at other industries operating in the region. Textiles was a sunset industry back in the

States and I'd have to find something new anyway. My résumé was packed with experience with Asia businesses, so I decided to leverage that expertise to help me change industries.

But even more powerful than my credentials was ... well, Lori. She had made such fast friends with the soccer players extraordinaire, Steve and Doreen, that they did not want us to leave China. Steve, who was general manager at TE Connectivity, a company that manufactured connectors and sensors for automobiles, ended up recruiting me to join the company. Although I was fortunate to have a few offers, I accepted Steve's invitation and was officially hired by Jeff Bartlett, the VP of operations, and I became director of operations strategy, with the idea in mind that I would succeed Jeff in a year. After only three weeks on the job, however, Jeff was pulled away to the consumer side of the business, which involved supervising eleven other plants in China. Suddenly, I was promoted to VP of operations, reporting directly to Steve! You can't move up the ladder much faster than that, so I guess I didn't mess up too badly.

Even though I was no longer supervising textiles, I quickly discovered that the language of manufacturing is the same no matter what you're making. You had to pay attention to the five main drivers—safety, on-time delivery, quality, productivity, and engagement. So the spreadsheets are the same.

However, the language of communicating in China was, of course, very different. But this was another gap I was determined to address. And that involved taking another big risk.

My Mandarin Meeting

After starting my position at TE, I had to prepare for my first town hall meeting with some two hundred Chinese factory workers. I thought about how to best create a bond with them. After all, they didn't know me from Adam—I was the new kid on the block and wanted to find a way to show them I was respectful of them and their culture. I decided the best way to do that was speak *their* language, which was Mandarin Chinese.

I wasn't going from zero to sixty-five when I made this choice—for years, I had been listening to Chinese language tapes in my car because I had to deal with people in that country so much when they began to take over textile manufacturing. Then, I had to up my game when we made the move to China. I mean, my driver didn't speak a word of English! I had to at least get better at giving directions. I hired a private tutor and took weekly lessons. I posted notes around our apartment, showing me how to say everyday words and phrases, like *saucepan* and *jacket in my closet*. I began to know just enough Mandarin to be dangerous.

> I was the new kid on the block and wanted to find a way to show them I was respectful of them and their culture.

However, I knew doing the entire town hall in Mandarin was going to be another huge challenge. The language is very tonal. A word can have three completely different meanings based on what part you emphasize in its pronunciation. Being a southern US boy by upbringing, a drawl was natural to my way of speaking. However, that placed me in dangerous territory when using the words for such ideas as quality, delivery, productivity, and safety for the first time in Mandarin. What would happen if I said the wrong thing? What if I accidentally said a dirty word and everyone laughed at me?

When you take a risk, you need to mitigate it as much as possible. So I needed a plan to make sure what I said would (a) make sense and (b) wouldn't insult anyone.

With that in mind, I wrote out my entire presentation in English. My Mandarin tutor translated it, and then I recorded her reading it. From that recording, I learned the pronunciations of problematic words and took pages of notes to help me keep them in mind. I practiced alongside her recording many times. I also created the PowerPoint deck for the presentation in both English and Mandarin. This way, if I did mispronounce something, the audience could read for themselves and see what I was struggling to say.

When it came time for the town hall, I experienced something remarkable—I actually received a round of applause after every single sentence I spoke during that half-hour presentation. I had to continually pause for their clapping between every slide. It was evident they knew what an effort I had made, and they were determined to show their appreciation for that effort every way they could, because I was the first expat to do that kind of thing. Meeting them halfway brought me instant respect—and that in turn empowered my engagement with them as well as support for my brand of servant leadership. I showed them they were important and that I wasn't going to be the "Ugly American" who insisted on everything being done his way. I truly underestimated how important this gesture was to them.

This was an auspicious beginning to my new career in China. I never imagined when I was a boy growing up in a small town in Georgia that one day I would be speaking Mandarin to two hundred Chinese employees. That moment in my life would never have come if I hadn't taken the massive risk of moving us all to China. I was empowered because I made the big move and embraced inevitable change instead of fighting it. Because I did take that risk, I not only grew personally, but those in my orbit did as well.

I'll tell you about that in the next chapter.

CHAPTER 8

Empowered by
CHANGE

Sometimes, when you completely change up your environment, great things can happen. You're challenged in ways you never were before; you access new skills and knowledge to meet those challenges, and that can't help but force you to grow as a person. Winston Churchill once said, "To improve is to change; to be perfect is to change often." I know that's the case with me, although I can't say I'm perfect (an assessment my family would agree with!).

In the last chapter, I talked about how living in China made me rise to the occasion. But I wasn't the only one. Lori also expanded her horizons. She is someone who never met a stranger—I already related how strongly she bonded with our fellow expats, Steve and Doreen, and how that not only led to a lifetime friendship but also my new career. She didn't stop there, though. Almost overnight, she had put together a group of international friends to do things with. They took Chinese language classes together and held informal "club" meetings. And when the weekend rolled around, I just turned to her and asked her what we were going to be doing—she always had a great plan put together.

Professionally, she wasn't allowed to teach in China—you had to be a citizen of that country to be in the public school system. Instead, she volunteered to teach English at a charity school for the children of migrant workers. And she ended up becoming the equivalent of a PTA president for my son's high school in Shanghai!

And speaking of Austin, I want to relate how the China experience actually helped him academically.

Getting Schooled in Shanghai

Now, you might have gotten the impression that Austin struggled in school from that last statement. Far from the truth. As I mentioned, he did very well in school in the States. In junior high, he made straight As. But here's the weird part about that …

Back in America, I never saw the boy do any homework.

My takeaway from that was he wasn't being sufficiently challenged in our small town's school. If he was getting all As and never had to study, something was off. But what could I do about it? If he was doing that well, I couldn't really complain about the situation.

In Shanghai, his new school proved to be very, very different. When he entered as a freshman, its academic ranking of all schools who used the North American education model was eleventh … out of ninety thousand. In other words, Austin was suddenly in a *very* demanding academic environment, and he had to adjust accordingly. That meant homework. Lots of it.

Every weeknight when I came home from work, we'd have our family dinner and do our "highs and lows" (as discussed in chapter 1). Then both Austin and I would just keep on working. I would go into my home office for evening conference calls back in America, since that's how the time zones lined up. Meanwhile, Austin would go do his studies in his room. We would both keep going until it was bedtime. We were a couple of very busy boys!

At first, he was resistant to learning Chinese, but I pushed him a bit on it, and he ended up being very fluent. The time in China also did our relationship a lot of good, because I got to spend a lot of time with him, where before, back in the States, I was traveling all the time.

I was proud of how he adapted to his new situation and made it work for him. However, he was a teenager, and teenagers do things. In China, there is no official drinking age, at least there wasn't at that time. Basically, if you could get your chin above the bar and you had the money, they would pour you a drink. Anyway, Austin was fifteen; we didn't allow him to drink, but he had some friends who were older. If he was out with them, I would always stay up and keep working until he got home, while Lori went to bed.

> I was proud of how he adapted to his new situation and made it work for him.

One night during our first year there, he came home a little … well, not quite right. He wasn't 100 percent, if you know what I mean. So I asked him point blank, "Have you been drinking?" He replied, "Oh no, Dad, no, no, no." I said, "All right, go to bed."

The next morning, he came down and quickly apologized for lying to me. Then he explained to me what had been going on. There was some kind of celebration, and all his friends were giving him a hard time for not partying the way they were partying. He gave in to the peer pressure and took a couple of shots.

I had to say, "Well, son, if your friends want to make you do that sort of thing, then you're just not going to be able to go out with them. They have to understand you're not allowed to drink." I didn't have another issue with him after that.

Flash forward to when Austin was seventeen, about two years later.

I received a text from him saying, "I'm out at a birthday party. Would it be okay if I had one beer?" I told him yes. From then on, he would let me know if he was going to have a drink, but he never came home drunk again. I could trust him, even when he went on to college, because he was no longer the kid who never had a drink. He knew what it could do and how to control his consumption.

Austin had some tremendous experiences during our time in China. Because of the way the school system was plugged into a network, he was given the opportunity to travel for music and sports events. That enabled him to hit a grand slam at a Hong Kong baseball competition, as well as do music he loved, as he is a gifted singer and plays a couple of instruments. At the end of our time in China, his passport had stamps from the aforementioned Hong Kong, as well as Tokyo, Seoul, Manila, Kuala Lumpur, Amsterdam, London, Dubai, and several other Chinese cities. I told him it would've taken the rest of his life to get that many stamps if we hadn't moved to China.

When Austin graduated from high school in China, he had five best friends—an American, a German, an Indian, someone from Hong Kong, and someone from China. He never would've had such a diverse set of friends back in North Carolina. He ended up going to Lehigh University for mechanical engineering with a minor in—guess what?—Chinese. He made dean's list for four years and won what's called a Presidential Scholarship, which allowed him to attend Lehigh for another year for free (except for room and board) to get his master's degree in mechanical engineering. He did so and achieved that degree while earning a 4.0 GPA.

Am I proud of my son? Is the grass green?

Lily

Now, I want to turn the tables. I want to talk about how America empowered a very special young lady, simply because she made the same kind of cultural switch as Austin—with my help.

This story happened back in this timeline a bit, back when I first began traveling to Asia for business. I arrived in Shanghai Pudong International Airport for the very first time and encountered what I considered the true definition of well-managed chaos. Looking down into the terminal, it looked like someone had kicked down an anthill and its residents were left scurrying around every which way. ("Ants Marching" is one of my favorite Dave Matthews Band songs. Oh, and, of course, *Back in Black* by AC/DC may be the greatest album of all times … but I digress.)

My purpose for the trip was simple. I was there to set up a China-based supply chain to resource low-cost commodity textiles in Asia. Jerry, a US-based office furniture customer and friend, had established a sourcing resource in China and offered to make the introductions for me—we had intended to connect in Chicago and fly together to Shanghai. But I arrived there all alone—Jerry had gotten the flu and bailed on me at the last minute.

I navigated China's customs on my own—which, believe me, was not an easy task for a first timer. This was in the days before international cell phone access, so I did not even have contact information for the sourcing company we were supposed to meet with. I didn't know how to get in touch with anyone. I tried to think of a plan B and came up with nothing. Finally, I discovered an airport hotel within walking distance—I decided to crash there and fly back to the US the next day. I began looking for a way out of the terminal, when all of a sudden I heard a voice calling my name:

"Mr. Rice! Mr. Rice!"

I turned to see a Taiwanese man, two Chinese men, and a Chinese teenager, a girl. One Chinese man was the business owner and the father of the teenager. The other Chinese man was their driver. Neither spoke any English, but, fortunately, the Taiwanese and the teenage girl did, and very well, as my Chinese language skills were limited to what I had retained from the language tapes I had listened to in the car back home.

The business owner's name was Mr. Zhou, and we became fast friends despite the language barrier. Over the next few years, his family-led business empowered me to accomplish my task of developing a reliable Asian supply chain. They made introductions to manufacturing companies and qualified supplier candidates, oversaw quality control, processed orders, and arranged shipping logistics. Over the course of time, I helped them solve technical textile questions and more effectively address the quality expectations of the North American markets. And after the regular business model ran its course, we remained in contact, as I provided advice on several of their challenges dealing with US-based customer demands.

At this point, Mr. Zhou's daughter, who was named Lena but used Lily for her American name, was going to college in Canada. Mr. Zhou obviously loved his girl but also despaired about his situation. This was when families in China were only allowed to have one child legally, and since Mr. Zhou didn't have a son, he was concerned he would not have an heir to take over the family business when he retired. At that time, many traditional Chinese businessmen would not even discuss business with a female!

To me, the solution was obvious. After she completed college, I offered this young, bright adult a job in North Carolina in the textile business working in customer service. Her language skills and understanding of the business positioned her perfectly to deal with our international customer and supply base. At the same time, this position afforded her the opportunity to learn more about American culture and the Western way of doing business.

She worked in the position for two years and then returned home, having proven herself as a capable businesswoman. I like to think that in some small way I helped empower her to break the traditional gender barriers and successfully succeed her father in leading their business. She would have found it extremely hard going to get a foothold in business back in China. Working for me, however, helped her avoid all the roadblocks and get the experience she needed to earn the respect of Chinese businesspeople.

Lily also became a wife and mother back in her home country. When she was married, it was the biggest wedding I had ever attended, with six hundred people in attendance surrounded by what seemed like a million flowers. Today, she runs the family business, which remains very successful—the father has semiretired. And every year for Christmas, she sends me a $500 gift card.

But that's not all Lily has gifted me with.

Let's do another time jump to February of 2020, when our world seemed to change almost overnight due to the COVID-19 global pandemic. As you might recall, hospitals, businesses, and individuals all across America were scrambling to get personal protective equipment (PPE). Demand was skyrocketing. Because most PPE came from Asia, it was almost impossible to get at the start of the pandemic.

Well, the next month, a large box showed up at the plant in Wisconsin I was running at the time (more on that in the next chapter), and what was inside was a huge surprise. I had been sent a shipment of five hundred KN95 masks from China as a gift. Yes, Lily, now running the family business, had sent them to me as a gift, knowing I would need them. That was just the start. She had a qualified supply chain, and soon I was able to source over one hundred thousand more masks to support my business as well as the others in our private equity portfolio at a time when other companies just had to do without. Me, I had boxes stacked all the way to the ceiling of my office. I would break them down myself, split them up to get them to those who needed them, then get them boxed up to send out. I was even able to send some KN95 masks to a hospital when their supply was exhausted.

I always find it amazing how relationships built along your journey can sometimes stand the test of time. Because I empowered Lily, now a business leader and mother, she empowered me to provide PPE solutions to my company and others when supply options were extremely limited. To this day, we connect at least once a year to share family pictures and share the blessings for a prosperous new year.

When my son was graduating from high school, we knew it was time to return home. The experience had been amazing, but our pool of friends was rapidly shrinking—expats tended to be on the move more than most—and we hadn't been very aggressive in making new ones. However, we had gotten a tremendous amount of empowerment from this extreme change of countries and cultures. And we all came out the better for it.

CHAPTER 9

Empowered by
TEAMWORK

Teamwork is an essential element of empowerment.

I've had a lot of experience with that concept. From being the captain of a football team to running a manufacturing plant, from joining a powerlifting team to being part of a fraternity, I love other people and the empowerment that comes from everyone working together to achieve amazing goals.

Together is the key word in that last sentence. You can be working with a bunch of people, but if they're all at each other's throats, you're not going to make much progress. That's why I'm a firm believer in servant leadership. By being sensitive to people's needs and removing obstacles that stand in the way of their success, you open the door to your own. And everyone involved accomplishes a whole lot more than they could have on their own.

I've been lucky enough to be a part of more than a few successful teams. And the story I want to tell you in this chapter is about how I brought together an amazing group to create amazing results, because to me, it illustrates perfectly how teamwork empowers us all to get the job done.

The Founder Who Fled to Hilton Head

Around the beginning of 2017, I was looking for a new opportunity. My relationship with my new boss at TE Connectivity wasn't the best, and we both agreed it wasn't working out. He kept me on to run things until I found a new place to land.

At this point, I was looking for a change anyway. More specifically, I was eager to engage with the world of private equity. Private equity firms buy companies for the purpose of increasing their value and then selling them at a profit five years down the line—that's how they make money. But one thing these firms do not want to do is run those companies themselves, as they don't have that expertise. They either leave the acquisition's leadership in place after a sale goes through—or hire someone qualified to take over who could continue to make the business work. I was hoping to be the latter. I felt running one of those acquired properties could be a new challenge for me and one I'd enjoy.

A recruiter I had known for about twenty years connected me with Morgenthaler Private Equity, a firm that had been formed in 1968 by David Morgenthaler, a successful Cleveland-based entrepreneur. The company had evolved over the years and, in 2012, it was rebranded as MPE by three new partners who established funds and a portfolio dedicated to lower middle market private equity investments. One of their recent acquisitions—PCI, which stood for Plastic Components Inc.—needed new leadership, and I was selected for the job.

PCI specialized in plastic injection molding and was based in Germantown, Wisconsin, where Lori and I moved for the duration of my tenure there. Tom Duffy was the founder/owner of PCI and had opened it up for business roughly thirty years earlier. Tom was a classic entrepreneur who was now approaching sixty and told me straight up when I met with him that the business had outgrown him. He had begun the company with just two presses and a handful of sample orders and grew it into a great business. What had been a simple business to run had, however, grown increasingly complex as a result, and he felt it was now too big for him to manage; he just didn't have that kind of experience. I respected his honesty and his awareness that it was time for new management. What I didn't realize was this transition was about to cause his emotions to boil over.

That happened while I was on site for the second time. I was talking with his HR manager (who had been with him for twenty years, as had his head of sales and marketing) in her office. Tom stuck his head in the door, said something I can't remember to the HR manager, and left.

And I mean *left*.

His people never saw him again. They never spoke to him again. He had simply flown off to his winter home in Hilton Head to lick his wounds. The truth was he couldn't deal with separating himself from the company he had spent so much time and energy building. To him, if he was no longer leading the whole shebang, he didn't want to be involved at all. After the sale went through, he was still leading the company (not that unusual with a private equity purchase, as continuity of leadership is important to those types of buyers), but MPE expected more of him than he was prepared to deliver. He openly admitted he had never prepared a budget or forecast in the past. And when he had to prepare for his first board of

> I respected his honesty and his awareness that it was time for new management.

directors meeting with MPE, it was an enormous struggle. He wasn't used to being accountable to others, it was always his shop, and he was rattled by the prospect of presenting to the board. I was told he practiced doing his presentation about twenty times, and it still didn't go real well.

Around that time, MPE offered me the role of president/CEO. I only chafed at one of their asks—that I commit to becoming a Green Bay Packers fan, since they were based in Wisconsin! Well, whatever it took …

After Tom did his vanishing act, he left a lot of emotional baggage behind. After all, he had just completely severed decades-old relationships with his people in a heartbeat—and those people were left stunned by his abrupt exit. I could tell they were shaken, and I knew I had to restore some faith in their roles and create some confidence in my leadership moving forward.

This kind of situation is where building trust is so important. One of my favorite books, *The Speed of Trust*, by Stephen Covey, makes the point that trust is "the most overlooked, misunderstood, underutilized asset to enable performance. Its impact, for good or bad, is dramatic and pervasive. It's something you can't escape." I feel the same way. Hopefully, as you have seen throughout this book, I'm not the kind of guy who comes in stomping his feet and breathing fire—my approach is to use my position to create positive and productive relationships, respect everyone equally, and avoid flexing my authority arbitrarily.

So, as I faced my first board of directors meeting (fortunately, I was more than familiar with them—I only had to do one walk-through prior to the meeting), I did what I could to show confidence in my department heads. I trusted them to give an accurate update on performance and priorities in their areas of supervision—and they did. I soon grew to appreciate the team I'd inherited. And, by the way, we never had to practice for a board meeting again.

I'd like to now walk you through my five-year journey at PCI, which was a totally new experience because I had a finite amount of time to build the value of the business in order for the private equity firm to sell it at a good profit. The following case study is how I was able to meet that goal (spoiler alert!).

2017, Year 1—Establishing Trust

As I began to successfully bond with the people at the plant, I started to consider the challenge I had before me. As I said, when private equity firms buy companies like PCI, it's typically with an eye to grow its value as high as possible and then sell after five years. I had to boost PCI's worth by then, or their investment was for naught.

On day ten of assuming my leadership role, I took the team off site, and we spent a few days getting aligned. I tried to create strong engagement in order to get everyone on the same page. Then we began to create a living document that would represent our strategic map for increasing company worth over the next few years. After a few follow-up sessions, that document was finished. We would revisit it every four to six months to make sure we were progressing as we wanted, but mostly we used it as our guide when we dealt with the tactical day-to-day stuff.

This kind of high-level planning was all new to my team, especially when I shared PCI's financials. When I stepped in, they didn't really know how the company was doing. People knew it was successful, but they didn't know *how* successful. Simply put, there wasn't much transparency. There were no communication protocols or town halls. Apparently, Duffy just kept all that to himself—as I said, he was old school.

Yes, it was bad, all that had been missing from management up until then. What was good, however, was that I had the opportunity to put them into place, along with a few other important changes, such as the implementation of plant-wide and company-wide incentive programs that sent the message "Everybody wins or nobody wins." I also put in nine TVs around the plant. The top left-hand corner always showed how the plant was performing, and it was updated on a monthly basis. The rest of the screen featured company news, things like birthdays, customer visits, the latest quality issues, that kind of stuff. It was a way to visually convey information to everybody and make them all feel they were part of a community. Sharing the performance numbers was a way for everyone to see how close to getting that incentive bonus they were.

Employee engagement was very much on my mind, so I also established what I consider to be its basics—performance reviews, town hall meetings, lunch-and-learn programs, and a safety program. We also began doing service awards, onboarding videos, and company newsletters, as well as offering 401(k) matching, life insurance, and competitive healthcare benefits. The result was we ended up being recognized by *Plastic News*, our industry's trade publication, as one of the best places to work, an honor we continued to receive every year after that while MPE maintained ownership (later on, in 2020 and 2021, right smack in the middle of COVID, we took first place).

My next step was to engage with our customers. We created an effective "customer road show" and then went on the road to present it to all our key accounts. Just as I had to ease the anxiety of my own team about the change in leadership, I now had to make our biggest customers feel at ease by reassuring them that the new private equity ownership wasn't going to cause us to lose our focus. There are a lot of bad stories about private equity firms buying companies and then stripping them down—destroying the existing value. If you've ever seen the movie *Wall Street*, you know what I'm talking about. But I would never have taken this job if that had been MPE's plan. So I had to explain to them that MPE was a "buy and build" firm. We would remember what got us to where we were and grow from that foundation to move forward.

That's all the good stuff. But there were some difficult times in the beginning as well.

Our senior engineer, Rich, was tremendously respected and very well liked. He was very active in his church, big in youth development, and did Habitat for Humanity projects in different parts of the country. He was also a motorcycle rider. He left a little late one night just as it was getting dark. A deer jumped out in front of him; he swerved to avoid the animal, and hit a dump truck head-on. He was killed in that collision. Our team had never been through anything like that, and we got through that tragic event together. We created a GoFundMe page for his family and even a lot of our customers contributed to it. We also helped his family finish a house renovation project that he had started and renamed our main conference room in his honor. We did what we could, but there was no way to paper over the fact that everyone had experienced a major loss with his passing.

Then, on the business side, we lost two major customers that had provided some of our highest profit margins—they ended up sourcing in-house, so it wasn't like we had done anything wrong. But it was obviously a big blow to the bottom line. It meant that before I really started to make any big moves, I was already underwater in terms of the growth-and-margin-performance story that we were attempting to create.

I didn't panic; I was just determined to keep at it. I believe this kind of challenge brings out the best in me, and I found myself stepping up my game to the highest level. That in turn motivated everyone else to step up their game. Tony Raffo, the big Italian I spoke of earlier in this book, used to tell me that if the captain looks nervous, then the crew thinks the ship is going down. I wasn't going to send that message, so I tried to remain cool and confident.

What we had to do was build a sales pipeline that would deliver more customers and more revenue. This was more new territory for the company. My sales manager (who had been Tom Duffy's sales manager) told me that over his twenty years at PCI, he never had to report on what he had sold or forecast what he would sell. These were essential sales skills I had to teach him as well as his sales staff so they would be set up to succeed.

2018, Year 2—Acquisitions

I had accomplished most of my goals for year one. I felt I was successful in getting the team in place and trained for institutional leadership. My objective with that team (and pretty much every team I've led) was to work myself out of a job. What do I mean by that? Well, if you build the support structure in such a way that your people understand what they have to do and what they have to work toward, they are more than capable of running things without you—especially if they're the right people. Most like being given that degree of freedom to do their jobs anyway, so once you establish all the parameters ... well, you don't have to spend all your time looking over their shoulders.

That freed me up to pursue some potential M&A (mergers and acquisitions) opportunities.

One of the tactics private equity firms employ to quickly build up the value of a business like PCI is to acquire other small companies that complement it and create profitable synergy—these are called *add-ons* in the private equity world. To identify potential add-ons, I joined up with the biggest trade association in our industry, the Manufacturing Association of Plastic Processors, where I was named to its board of directors and eventually became VP of the association.

As I increased my knowledge of the industry, I, along with my CFO and key board members, began to map out a solid acquisition strategy for us and spent a lot of time visiting potential companies that seemed to fit in with that strategy. I personally visited over forty of them, while maybe another twenty, hearing that I was looking to buy, came to visit me.

Our criteria for these purchases had four main points. One was geographic—since PCI was already located in the Midwest, we wanted to expand to each coast. A second was that the companies had to have a reasonable profit margin—we were already a strong financial performer, and we didn't want an add-on to dilute that success. Third, the companies had to bring new technologies into our portfolio so we would be able to expand our own capabilities. Finally, we wanted to increase the diversification of customers. When I first became CEO of PCI, the plumbing industry represented roughly 70 percent of our business. When I left, it represented only 28 percent of our business, and no customer was responsible for more than 20 percent of our revenue. Big difference.

2019, Year 3—Integration

After sending out four LOIs (letters of intent), we finally closed on our first acquisition, Syracuse Plastics of North Carolina, which was located in Cary, North Carolina, a couple of hours from our home in Elkin (I got some grief from the board about that—they thought maybe I was looking for companies near our old home on purpose!). We then changed the name of the facility to PCI Cary NC.

Once you do purchase a company that complements your main business, your work is far from done. The first challenge was to integrate PCI Cary into MPE's portfolio of companies. They had a model to make that happen, which they called their one-hundred-day plan. The one-hundred-day plan was represented by a lengthy spread-

> Once you do purchase a company that complements your main business, your work is far from done.

sheet that came out of the due diligence process categorized by functions that needed improvements, such as finance, IT, HR, operations, and whatever else needed to be addressed after the acquisition was final. That spreadsheet provided the tasks and timelines we were meant to accomplish, and we knocked it all out very, very aggressively and very seamlessly. We ended up getting everything done before those one hundred days were up.

The beauty of this add-on acquisition was how complementary it was to our home base in Wisconsin. The plant in Wisconsin was high volume, low labor. Much of it was automated. We didn't use operators because all the plant equipment was monitored and self-operating. Once you set it up, it ran on its own. Our weak point? We were not like Burger King in that we did not do special orders—if something needed to be done to individualize a product after it was finished, we didn't handle that. We kept it simple as well as efficient, manufacturing items that were easily boxed and shipped, because nothing we made was bigger than a football.

Our new acquisition in North Carolina was the opposite. They made very, very large parts and would do multiple changes after the fact if they were requested. Now we no longer had to turn down those kinds of customers as we had been doing—the Cary plant could do them for us. Right off the bat, some of our top customers traveled down to that facility, qualified them, and gave them business.

To run the Cary plant, we used a matrix style of management. That's when employees report to multiple bosses rather than one, and those bosses line up according to functions and project lines. For example, HR and sales in both plants connected to each other, even though there were general managers in place who still ran the individual facilities.

We also had the Cary plant go through the same integration plan we had completed after MPE took over the Wisconsin plant. Like that facility, the Cary company had been owned and managed by the founder since its inception, which was almost forty years ago—so they also had a lot to learn, and I was happy to help show them the way. They put together a value creation model for themselves, and then did their own SWOT analysis (strengths, weaknesses, opportunities, threats) as well as their own mission statement. I facilitated and supported those processes but gave them control. To me, it had to be homegrown. I also implemented the incentive compensation plan, like we had put in place at the host site.

While I started an outside search for a general manager for the Cary plant, I decided, after spending about three weeks with Durwood, the head operations guy, that he could do the job. He seemed to be the one really running the place and doing a good job at it. It was the best decision I made in this integration process. He became probably my closest friend from that entire group of executives I encountered during that time period. He's still doing a great job there and has taken on additional responsibilities.

2020, Year 4—Pandemic

The best laid plans of mice and men …

The pandemic, as you will probably recall, seemed to hit overnight in March of that year. When April rolled around, all our orders were suddenly getting canceled. Customers were also closing down for the duration. We had to figure out how to manage all this chaos and keep our own doors open.

Luckily, one of our West Coast customers manufactured ventilators. Because we made components for them, we could justifiably assert that we were a critical business, even as other businesses went on lockdown. All our employees had to keep government paperwork with them in case they got pulled over on their way into the plant by an officer who was supposed to make sure companies were shut down. We had the official green light to keep on going.

Because we were owned by private equity, we didn't qualify for the PPE loans. But our CFO was very aggressive in researching other options, and we ended up getting government help through state and federal unemployment programs in order to provide our workers with full pay, even though they had reduced work schedules. Nobody in the company lost money during that time frame. I was the guy who, for the first time in his life, had to file for unemployment because of *my* reduced work schedule!

We also put together robust protocols for plant safety and cleaning. I had some major help in that regard from an unexpected source. If you remember my story about Lily in the last chapter, you'll remember she sent me that amazing gift of boxes and boxes of masks from China. We then required that if you were going to be in the plant, you had to wear one of those masks.

We got some pushback on that, as many businesses did. One day I was walking through the plant, masked as I should be, when a toolmaker came up to me and said, "Derrill, I got a problem with these masks; let me tell you why."

I said, "All right, what's your problem, Tom?"

"Well, I've done the research, and the particle that is a virus is *XYZ* 0.777, but the mask only filters through point *C* or 0.005, and therefore the particle gets through the mask. And so the mask doesn't really do you any good."

My reply? "Well, I'm going to give you five reasons why you need to wear it. First of all, the particle itself is not the transmission vehicle—it's the moisture that carries the particle. So when I talk, there's moisture coming out of my mouth. That's the transportation vehicle for that viral component, and this mask does filter moisture. Second, the mask is more to protect others than it is to protect you, because when you're talking while you're infected, you are sending out those viral particles in the moisture that goes along with your speaking. Third, it's out of respect. It's like if I go to a park, sit on a bench, and start smoking a cigar, and I see there's a family downwind of me sitting on a blanket on the grass, opening up their lunch baskets and getting ready to eat. I'm not going to smoke that cigar just out of respect because I don't want my smoke going into that family's picnic. Fourth, if your colleague over there were to get sick from COVID, and the insurance company finds out that we're not enforcing the mask mandate that was in place at the time in the state of Wisconsin, we could be liable if he gets deathly ill. So you're putting the whole company at risk."

So far, so good. The toolmaker was nodding along with me. Then I delivered the kicker.

"Finally, and most importantly, is number five—you either put on the mask or quit and go home."

I wasn't kidding. I've seen a lot of serious injuries where people were hurt who didn't have to be, and I didn't believe in taking foolish chances with people's lives.

Meanwhile, our largest customer filed for Chapter 11 due to their poor performance prior to the pandemic. That was another battle, because they owed us a lot of money. We ended up getting about 90 percent of what they owed us, because we told them we weren't going to ship product to them until they paid. That would've shut them down because they needed our parts to manufacture. That got their attention.

By September, the chaos of COVID-19 was finally beginning to settle down. The vaccine had been released, and mask mandates were starting to be eased. We took a three-day off-site retreat to get us back on track with our long-term strategy of value creation. It was invaluable. We came out of the pandemic whole. We didn't have to refinance or create a new debt structure, like so many others. Nor did we have to lose any employees. If anything, we needed more workers who were suddenly hard to find, so we had to ramp up our automation to compensate for that.

The bottom line, however, was we were back on track.

Year 5—The End of the Journey

It was now 2021. Business began to boom again. And because we kept our operation intact, we had the team and the capability to ramp right back up, which our customers noticed and appreciated. We also made our second acquisition, a plant in Utah, which gave us West Coast coverage. All of that was good for me, because MPE was nearing the end of the five-year journey with this investment. Which meant it was time to sell all three plants.

Midyear, we kicked off that sale process. We brought in an investment banker to represent the company in a sale and put together the financials. We began with a funnel of 149 targeted potential buyers and whittled that down over time to a handful of finalists. Most of them were financial buyers, bigger private equity groups who just wanted to keep making the money we were making from the plants and eventually sell again. But the one that stood out was Rosti, a strategic buyer who was in the same business as PCI but did not yet have a footprint in North America. That was the buyer we went with.

Afterward, the senior team of PCI as well as a few of the MPE executives and others involved in the sale all brought their spouses for a long weekend celebration in Napa Valley to celebrate an amazing five-year run. We ended up delivering about a 400 percent return to the stakeholders, the investors, and the private equity firm, who called our success a "hall of fame investment story."

I might sound like I'm bragging—and maybe I am a little, it's my book, after all!—but I cannot emphasize enough that I always bring along humility as my constant companion in my leadership approach. I also make sure my attitude is positive and aimed at empowering others to do their best. There is a quote I have hanging on my wall that sums it all up for me. It's from Pastor Charles Swindoll, and it goes like this:

> We ended up delivering about a 400 percent return to the stakeholders, the investors, and the private equity firm, who called our success a "hall of fame investment story."

"The longer I live, the more I realize the impact of attitude on life. Attitude, to me, is more important than facts. It is more important than the past, the education, the money, than circumstances, than failure, than successes, than what other people think or say or do. It is more important than appearance, giftedness, or skill. It will make or break a company … a church … a home. The remarkable thing is we have a choice every day regarding the attitude we will embrace for that day. We cannot change our past

... we cannot change the fact that people will act in a certain way. We cannot change the inevitable. The only thing we can do is play on the one string we have, and that is our attitude. I am convinced that life is 10% what happens to me and 90% of how I react to it. And so it is with you ... we are in charge of our Attitudes."

I've always tried to put my best foot forward by keeping the best attitude possible. That attitude extends to making the most of every situation. In the next chapter, I'll tell you about a couple of times where I did just that to make an impact. For instance, making a Ford car disappear right in front of the head of Ford ...

CHAPTER 10

Empowered by
CREATIVITY

C reativity is a funny thing. You come up with the right idea and you can change the world. To me, creativity enables a leap of thought and a leap of faith. Many times, you're connecting things that don't really belong together, but somehow, by combining them, you end up with something that is much more than the sum of its parts.

Steve Jobs had it right with his iconic "Think Different" ad campaign for Apple back in the late '90s, where he put the spotlight on such gamechangers and geniuses as Albert Einstein, Thomas Edison, Bob Dylan, and Jim Henson (and, of course, Jobs himself forever altered our tech landscape with his Apple innovations, such as the Macintosh, iPod, iPhone, and iPad). These are people who created ideas and products no one had ever thought of before—because they viewed the world in their own unique way.

While I sure as heck am not in the league of some of the names I just mentioned, I've always been excited to use creativity to create a bigger impact. That impulse probably sprang from me putting on my dishwashing show back at the pizza parlor, where I drew my first appreciative audiences. I suppose that brought out the "ham" in me, which led to me learning magic and performing it for others. My late friend Tim Wilson was also someone who inspired me to do some performing when we did some music gigs together when I was a teenager. These experiences were incredibly fun and, more importantly, taught me the importance of grabbing an audience's attention by entertaining them any which way you could—even if you're just scrubbing plates!

So yes, there is a part of me that caught the showbiz bug and never shook it. While I never thought seriously about becoming any kind of performer (I was too practical for that), I did manage to bring that aspect of my personality into play to create some memorable moments in the business world that created a wow factor.

> These experiences were incredibly fun and, more importantly, taught me the importance of grabbing an audience's attention.

In this chapter, I want to relate a couple of those incidents where creativity really empowered me to go way beyond the parameters of the normal business get-together and create success for all concerned. In these two anecdotes, you'll see how I brought a sparkle of showmanship into the buttoned-down business world—much to the surprise of my audiences!

Where'd the Ford Go?

For the first story, let me take you back to when I worked for Milliken, my first employer out of college. I'll start with the back story—in the late '70s and early '80s, international manufacturing was starting to outstrip the US in quality, leading to a drop in our country's competitive edge. If you're old enough, you'll remember this is when Japanese cars were regarded as being superior to our American ones. Naturally, this caused considerable concern. Our government as well as the business world began to look for ways to tip the scales back in our favor.

In 1987, the US Congress established the National Quality Award, similar to one Japan gave out at the time, to honor the companies that produced the best-made products. The idea was this kind of recognition would hopefully motivate our manufacturers to boost their standards. The awards were named for Malcolm Baldridge, the secretary of commerce who had died tragically that year in an unexpected accident. The first ones were presented in November of 1988 by then President Ronald Reagan. Most expected cutting-edge high-tech companies would be the front-runners for this honor. Year one, that was the case.

Year two, however, *we* won.

It was a genuine upset. Milliken, a textile company, considered an old school, parochial business with not much of a tech base, came out on top. Yes, a great honor, but also a great responsibility. I was one of four pursuit of quality directors, each of us representing one of the Milliken divisions—the division I represented was automotive fabrics—and after we won the award, we were tasked with doing a weekly dog and pony show in our customer center. The customer center was built like a theater, with a real stage that had all the accoutrements of the real thing—curtains, lights, and all the rigging. You could do almost anything you could do on a Broadway stage. It also had one more thing important to this story—the stage also contained a big rotating platform, the kind of thing you might see in a fancy showroom.

Every week, we would have to demonstrate what we did to win the award—and how we did it—to an audience of about a hundred executives from all types of industries. Our vice president of quality would then do a more detailed presentation on the main floor. Now, about that VP—he was a little bit of a nut. By that I mean he would wear silly outfits and try to do some funny stuff with his talk to make it a little more entertaining. And I have to admit that he may have inspired me to step it up a bit.

The reason I wanted to step it up was that I was told that Edsel Ford II, then head of the Ford Motor Company (whose slogan at the time was "Quality Is Job One") was coming to see what we were all about, since we had just won this major award. Because I was the pursuit of excellence director for our automotive division, I felt the burden of that upcoming visit more than my peers. This wasn't going to be for one hundred executives, like the other presentations—it was just going to be him and his staff, about ten people in all, for our audience.

I knew he would want to have a high-level conversation with the top level of management here. That meant I probably wouldn't have much of an interaction beyond a simple *hello*, if even that. At the same time, I wanted to make a good impression on him since we would be doing our stage show first.

And suddenly I remembered watching a David Copperfield special that gave me a brainstorm. This was back when he would do massive illusions that were astonishing to TV viewers. In this hour show, he had a Learjet on the tarmac at an airport, surrounded by people who dropped huge curtains around the aircraft so that it was obscured, but you could see the shadows of its outline and lights.

When those curtains dropped, the jet was gone!

Now, because I had studied magic, I was able to figure out just how David Copperfield had made that huge trick work. That's going to stay my secret. However, with that illusion in mind, I went to a Ford car lot and found their smallest compact car. I did some measurements on it and discovered that small car would indeed fit on our stage's turntable platform.

I spent a couple of weekends before Mr. Ford's visit building out the stage so I could make David Copperfield's illusion work here. When Mr. Ford and his contingent were there in the seats of the theater, we took down the lights and revealed the car at center stage. A couple of people came out with a huge frame that held a giant piece of fabric (frame built by yours truly) and put it up behind the car. The car, which had a spotlight on it, started to rotate on the turntable, and, as with the jet, you could still see the shadow of the car behind the fabric. We then put more frames of fabric around the car until it was completely obscured from view.

Then … suddenly … all the frames fell down at once, and, in the two seconds it took for that to happen, the car "vanished" into thin air. At that moment, a big banner came down from the top of the stage that read "Ford and Milliken, where quality is NO illusion." Mr. Ford was stunned and later told people that it was a very impressive start to the presentation.

It wasn't until all was said and done that I realized that if the trick hadn't worked, I might have looked like a real clown in front of those Ford bigwigs. Suppose those frames had come down with the car still sitting there? Maybe I would have been fired! I was so focused on making it work, I didn't even consider what would happen if it didn't. Luckily, it all went well and I remained employed! This was probably the riskiest project I ever took on in my entire career, but I didn't think about the risk at the time. I was just in the moment. Now it remains a very happy memory and a great example of how taking a creative leap can really pay off.

The Tonight Show Starring J. Derrill Rice

Now, let me share one more story along these lines. This stunt wasn't as big a risk, but it was just as much fun (if not more so!).

This happened when I was working for TE Connectivity, the company I went to work for in China. It had made a major acquisition in the industrial and commercial transportation space, and my boss had sponsored me to lead the business. Coordination was an interesting challenge. I was still living in Shanghai and so was our business strategy guy, but the head of sales was living in Germany, our operations leader was in California, and our HR and finance leaders were in North Carolina. We made it work. Weekly touch-point meetings and quarterly live strategy meetings at different locations around the world were key to ensuring alignment. This was another case where I empowered people to do their best, and they delivered—we ended up with the highest operating profit across all segments within the parent company.

At that time, TE Connectivity would have a global leadership meeting once every two years, and that meeting would also happen in different parts of the world. One might be in Lisbon, Portugal; the next one might be in Paris, France. We would have anywhere from five hundred to six hundred people in attendance at one of them. The intent of Steve (you remember Steve from chapter 7—my neighbor in Shanghai who recruited me) was to have each of his four business unit leaders, which included me, make a presentation on their business to a subset of the corporate gathering—the 250 members of our automotive segment. That way, everyone would see the highlights of all four of our business units. That year's global event was to occur close to home, in Orlando, Florida.

I quickly began working on my presentation. And I just as quickly became bored with what I was doing.

I was at the point in my career where I had made and sat through so many PowerPoint presentations that I would rather get stuck in the eye with a sharp stick than do another one! I wanted to do something different, something that would entertain people as well as educate them about our industrial and commercial transportation business unit inside the transportation segment of TE Connectivity. So I called Steve and asked him, "Do you mind if I change things up with my presentation?"

Steve asked what exactly I was planning.

"Well," I said, "I want to do it like *The Tonight Show* and have guests come on stage."

Steve knew me, he trusted me, and he agreed that I could take a shot at it.

So I followed the tried-and-true *Tonight Show* model to a *T*. With a nighttime city backdrop on the stage, similar to what every late-night talk show uses, my head of engineering introduced me like Ed McMahon used to do on the Johnny Carson show. I came out and did a monologue that basically roasted the transportation segment staff in a fun and harmless way.

From there, we went to a commercial—a short sales video about ICT. Then we brought out our first "guest," my financial guy, so I could show how we were power performing when it came to profits. He came out with a bunch of little beanbags with *ONE BILLION* printed on them (that was our revenue objective for the next year) and tossed them out to the audience. We then did the famous "Carnac the Magnificent" bit from Johnny Carson, with him reading the answers and me providing the questions.

From there, we showed another company video for a "commercial," and then I introduced our next guest, the head of sales and marketing. Since he was a Harley rider, he came out wearing a biker outfit, including leather pants! He did a bit about our matrix organization and put up a chart of all the people he used to report to (a couple of people) compared to whom he had to report to now (an *army* of people), which the audience died laughing at.

Then another commercial break, which I introduced as a look at our operational team. What we showed was an old Huggies commercial with a bunch of toddlers in diapers roaming around an office wearing neckties!

Then, back to the show. I explained our operational triumphs through a series of magic tricks utilizing three "volunteers" onstage. Then our head of distribution came onstage by crashing through a stack of boxes in a superhero costume! We made the point our distribution system was *so* good, we had everyone covered. Then I asked everyone in the audience to look under their chairs, where they found one of the components that I had made "disappear" during my magic show. I had gone into the theater the night before and put one under every one of the two hundred chairs in that room (now that's world-class distribution!).

Finally, my head of HR and my head of quality came out as our "musical guests." Our HR head dressed up as Tina Turner and lip-synched "Simply the Best," while our quality guy did "We Are the Champions," complete with air guitar! That was our big finish, and the audience began singing along at the top of their lungs.

> Instead of doing that through a series of dry PowerPoint slides, we did it by entertaining the audience.

Now, all that was fun, but each of the "segments" I had produced also had a point. They all conveyed ideas and information that I thought was important to present. But instead of doing that through a series of dry

PowerPoint slides, we did it by entertaining the audience. Everyone brought their A game. And I guarantee you this, at the end of that meeting, everybody in that dadgum room knew something about our business and how it was performing.

We had fun. We told a great story in a unique way. And this was only possible because Steve, my leader, empowered me to step out of the usual corporate box and do something creative that went beyond the standard dog and pony show. For this, I was recognized with the ICT Leadership Award—which was given only every two years. To this day, it's the most cherished recognition I have ever received, because it came from empowering my team to excel in a whole new way.

C H A P T E R   1 1

Empowered by
FAMILY

I'm at the age where I can truly appreciate how my family has empowered me over the years. Not only have they supported my career through all sorts of detours and disruptions, but they've also achieved so much on their own.

Lori, as I've said, is much more than a wonderful wife and mother; she's a remarkable woman with her own outstanding career. I mentioned how quickly she adapted to living in China and how she made her own life there. Well, when we moved to Wisconsin after I became the CEO of PCI, what I didn't mention is the toll it can take on a Southerner to move to that cold of a climate. However, again, she didn't blink. She began teaching at a Montessori school, and every morning, even in the winter, unless the temperature was below zero, the first forty-five minutes of the day were spent outside with the students on a farm that was located at the school. You want to wake up fast? Step out into the outdoors in January in Wisconsin!

As I noted in chapter 9, COVID-19 first struck while we were living there as well. To help Lori continue her important work, we turned our guest room into a teaching studio so she could teach online classes from home. After that turbulent time, she made the decision not to go back into the classroom, because she was actually getting asked to teach other teachers! So she earned her upper-level certificate for Montessori, and as of today, she's instructing teachers in two programs in Wisconsin and two programs in North Carolina.

Then there are our two wonderful kids. I have to be honest, when Lori and I tied the knot, we weren't sure we would ever have children. My aunt and uncle, who are now in their seventies, never had kids, so I saw it could work for a couple. And frankly, we were both a little anxious about parenting and whether we could do it well.

I ultimately think it was good to start off as husband and wife without putting ourselves under any time pressure on making that all-important decision. I guess it was around six or seven years into the marriage that she looked at me one night and said, "I think I'm ready to have kids." I simply said, "Okay, I'm in." We both knew it was time.

But we were still very nervous and maybe overcompensated for that. For example, when my wife was pregnant with Caroline, she would put this device on her stomach, kind of like a funnel with a tube, and ask me to talk through it so my daughter would recognize my voice when she came out. She also started doing flashcards with her when she was only three months old! By the time our son, Austin, came along, we weren't so obsessed about doing everything the exact right way—no funnels or flashcards that time. They weren't needed, apparently, because he grew up to be a fine young man who excelled at school.

We are so proud of what both kids have accomplished with their lives. Caroline is the most like me. Even before she could walk, she already acted like she was in charge of everything. Then, in high school, she became student body president, captain of the soccer team, homecoming queen, and valedictorian ... she rivaled my record! She's also a gifted actress and singer and starred in the musical *Annie* in elementary school. She also had her eye on bigger things than our small town had to offer. Between her junior and senior years, she did an honors program with the best students in the state—and she discovered she felt more at home with these high achievers than she did in her school at home in Elkin. Suddenly feeling like a big fish in a small pond, she applied to NYU, as well as a host of other colleges and universities.

Her final choice was between NYU and the University of North Carolina, and let me tell you, the difference in tuition was very substantial. The in-state school would be dramatically cheaper, but I knew her heart was leading her to NYU. I could see how conflicted she was, so I actually asked her to create a presentation on the pluses and minuses of both. She came through with a well-thought-out Power-Point, which did lay out those pluses and minuses—but I couldn't help noticing it was more than a bit biased toward NYU. However, at the end of the slide show, she said she couldn't ask the family to make that kind of financial sacrifice to send her there. I believe there was a tear or two in my eyes as I said, "Look, girl, as long as you get loans to pay for half of it, then we're in." She went to NYU and earned a degree in strategic marketing, with a focus on branding.

Each summer, she interned at a business in the Big Apple and ended up getting job offers from several of those companies when she neared graduation. For three years, she worked at a New York branding company, then, tiring of the concrete jungle, she moved to Denver to work for another branding firm there. Recently, she went out on her own and opened up her own business, with a focus on the hospitality industry.

As for Austin, he's more like his mom—very caring, but a quieter personality, not as much of an extrovert. As I related earlier, he went to Lehigh University, made dean's list, and earned his master's degree in mechanical engineering. He now lives in Seattle, working for Boeing, where he's been promoted three times, supervises others, and also mentors new hires.

We've had an incredible journey as a family, with love and support empowering all of us to make the most of every situation. We've all grown as a result. You might say all of us have aged like fine wine.

Oh, and speaking of wine …

Creating a Winery

There's a saying that if you want to make a million dollars, invest two million dollars in a winery. In other words, it ain't easy to make it work. Nevertheless, we created one and ran it as a family business.

Here's how that came to be.

I related how I came to take charge of the Chatham company back in chapter 5. That three-hundred-pound Italian I've mentioned before in this book recruited me to leave Milliken and join him on this adventure. It was a family-owned business until the Chathams decided to sell. I helped facilitate that sale, but the family assets didn't just include the actual manufacturing plant. There were three other properties that were owned by the company—a hunting lodge on an island off the coast of North Carolina, the grounds that had undeveloped housing plots on nine holes of the eighteen-hole local country club golf course,

> We've had an incredible journey as a family, with love and support empowering all of us to make the most of every situation.

and a property up the mountain that contained a complex of log cabins.

This last property had a rich history. It comprised three thousand acres on and around a creek called Grassy Creek, which feeds into the Yadkin River. It was initially developed in the 1920s by John Hanes of Hanes Hosiery fame (you may have heard of his underwear), together with J. C. Penney (you may have heard of his stores). They built the first log cabin there, as well a miniature version of the Hoover Dam to back up the creek and create an eight-acre lake. And then they used the turbine on that dam to power the cabin.

Mr. Chatham eventually bought out the Hanes and Penney families and continued to develop the property. In addition to expanding the main cabin, they built a couple of side cabins, a horse barn, a dog kennel, and a pheasant-raising area. One of his brothers decided to get into the dairy business around 1950, and they built a ten-thousand-square-foot dairy barn containing Guernsey cows, which were milking cows. The dairy farm became famous for its chocolate milk, which was known as the "sweetest in the land."

By the time I came along, the most important use of those cabins was to house guests of the Chatham company when they came to town. We renovated the cabins to make them a little more user friendly—after all, many of these guests were high-level customers from out of town. The cabins were necessary to solve a big problem for us—at the time, Surry and Yadkin Counties, where Elkin was located, were dry, so there were no upper-end hotels where we could put them up. The cabins were the answer.

I loved those cabins. But after a decade, the cabins no longer had value in terms of housing guests. The county loosened up the liquor laws, and now elite hotels felt it was a worthwhile investment to build in the area. That's why the next owners of the textile business chose not to buy the cabin complex. So now it was up for sale!

I was horrified when I heard a local group of developers wanted to buy the cabins' property in order to level the area and turn it into a residential subdivision. I had become emotionally connected to the cabins. When you walked into them, you could appreciate their original log cabin construction, complete with horsehair and hemp as the in-between insulation. All the logs had come from the property. The furniture, the pictures on the wall—they had all been there for fifty or sixty years. There were even antique muskets and pistols mounted on the walls.

So I made a decision based on pure emotion. I decided to try to save the property from those developers. I ended up winning it in a bankruptcy court in Delaware (a first-time experience for me). After I was successful, I came home and literally told Lori, "Honey, we just bought the farm." At the time, I felt like that dog who'd finally caught the car he was chasing. "Now what do I do with it?" was my thought.

For the past decade that property had been a second home to me, great for entertaining customers and enjoying the rich history of the place. Now it was owned by a bank with my name on the paperwork. And the mortgage was not chump change for me. It was time once again to get creative—and figure out something to do with all that land.

Let me skip back a few years, when I first began entertaining sophisticated customers from big cities. Well, I just didn't know what wine to order when I had a meal with them. I decided to rectify that hole in my knowledge base, so I put myself through a training class so I could understand that world a little better. I didn't get myself to a sommelier level, but I now knew enough to pick the wine at a dinner rather than asking the customer to do it. I even started my own wine cellar. So that seed was already planted.

The history of wine in North Carolina is an interesting one. Vineyards began to pop up in the early 1800s, due to the favorable soil and climate as well as the resiliency of the muscadine family of grapes, which were native to North Carolina. By 1840, the industry grew like wildfire, and soon this state was the largest wine producer in the country. Then prohibition shut it all down. That's when illegal moonshining took off, with hot rods transporting it all across county lines (if you ever watched the show *Dukes of Hazzard*, well, you're watching a little bit of history). Even after prohibition was finally over, the unlikely combination of moonshiners and protemperance church groups teamed up at the voting booth to create blue laws as well as keep some counties, such as ours, dry.

We could still *manufacture* wine, however (selling wine finally became legalized in the county in 2006). I discovered the soil on our property had some of the same properties of vineyard-friendly Northern California. Suddenly, I knew what I wanted to do with the land. There was a friend of mine, Jim Douthit, who had worked with me at Chatham and was talking about getting into the wine business. We decided to partner up. In April of 2003, we began planting our first ten acres of grapevines. We did it the hard way—with Jim driving a tractor that was pulling a tobacco planter that I sat in with my then six-year-old son, Austin, beside me in the well holding the vines and my daughter, Caroline, sitting on a nearby hill with a whistle, which she would blow whenever it was time to stick a new vine in the ground. When we heard that whistle, Austin would hand me a vine to stick in the ground and plant (later on, we used more sophisticated and easier planting methods!).

Creating a wine business from scratch was one time where I began to think I had bitten off more than I could chew, between the financial requirements and the challenges of the endeavor. The wine industry is really three businesses in one. The first is the farm, where you're constantly battling bugs, pestilence, fungi, birds, and deer to grow grapes. The winery itself is a manufacturing facility—it's all about chemicals and storage. The third business is in the hospitality sector—a tasting room, where you entertain guests. My wife and daughter favor the hospitality end. My son likes the winery the best. And the one thing we all agree on is we hate the vineyard the most—not even a close contest. It requires the hardest work.

Which led to an interesting conversation between me and my son when he was around eight years old. A bunch of us had been working in the vineyard all morning and finally took a lunch break. We were completely sweaty and filthy, sitting in our pickup truck, when Austin looked over at me. "Dad," he said, "I don't want this to come across the wrong way, but this is kind of a family business, isn't it?"

I nodded. "Well, yeah, it is."

He went on. "Okay, so when you guys pass away, it would go to the next generation, right?"

I nodded again. "Sure."

He thought for a minute. And then he looked at me again and said, "Dad, I really want to be clear about this. I want you to leave it to my sister."

"Why is that?" I asked.

"It's just way too much work."

"Well," I replied, "by that time, we'll hopefully have people in place to do most of that work. Maybe we'll have a vineyard manager and a tasting room manager. And since you'll already know everything about the business because you learned it from the ground up, you'll be able to oversee it all. You won't have to do all that hard work."

He thought for another minute.

"Still ... leave it to my sister."

You can't win 'em all.

The Case of the Holey Barrels

It took us a couple of years to do our first wine release of what we called our "Red Barn Blend." We only sold it by the case (we had enough for 350 cases) and only had an outdoor area for our sales, because our tasting room wasn't remodeled as of yet. As a matter of fact, we didn't even have any wine to taste, because we sold the cases in advance as a sort of preorder. And darned if we didn't sell it all before we even got any bottled. We called the winery "Grassy Creek" after the creek that runs through the property.

When we neared harvest time, we had to get oak barrels to store the wine in for those first 350 cases. We bought our first twelve, and I was a little shocked by how much they cost—$800 per barrel. We put them in the barn on a rail of four-by-four planks. And then a couple of weeks later, I noticed something. Under all the barrels were little piles of dust, almost in the shape of a bunch of little pyramids. I looked closer. Oh no. There were hundreds of tiny holes in the bottom of our barrels. Apparently, the barrels had awakened dormant oak borer beetles, and they immediately went to work drilling through our new and costly purchases.

The winery was at the point where it was costing me a lot, and I didn't want to see those barrels go to waste. So I put on my thinking cap and then went to a nearby Lowe's to buy some glasses that magnified whatever you were looking at. I also bought clippers, small rubber hammers, and boxes of toothpicks. With those supplies in place, Lori, the kids, and I went from barrel to barrel, finding the holes, tapping in toothpicks to plug them up and clipping off the ends of the toothpicks after they had been inserted. As I said, I'm talking hundreds of holes in each barrel, so this was no easy task (maybe this was the moment when Austin realized he wanted Caroline to inherit the business!). After we had the holes filled, we then filled the barrels with water to test them out. Usually, we would find a few holes that lurked under the metal bands of the barrels that we couldn't see without watching where the barrel was still leaking. We ended up saving all twelve barrels.

So a difficult beginning but a long-term success. Currently, we sell about four thousand cases per year, 99 percent of it right from the tasting room, which suits us just fine. We didn't want to have to jumpstart a distribution network, so we chose not to get any bigger. However, we were voted the best little winery in the Elkin Valley a couple of times and are often recommended as *the* winery to visit in North Carolina.

Are we making money? Well, as we say in the business world, we finally achieved a positive cash flow once we got over the hump of our debt load in 2019. And we still rent out the cabins, which was a great business during the start of the COVID pandemic—you could check into a cabin and leave without ever having to interact with anyone else!

But I didn't develop the property to make money. I did it to preserve the history of the area. And as an unexpected offshoot, it empowered our family to learn the strength of working together, persevering together, and sharing the pride of our accomplishments together. Right now, the winery for the most part runs on its own. I do drop in to work the tasting room, because I love to tell stories and entertain our visitors. I also help with the harvesting and bottling when I'm in town.

What kind of wine do we sell? Cabernet, Shiraz, merlot, chardonnay, pinot grigio, sauvignon blanc, and Riesling. But our biggest seller is a unique item, a 750-milliliter milk bottle with a picture of a cow on the front. In those milk bottles are our semisweet and dessert wines, sold under the name of Klondike Farm, the name of the original dairy farm that sold "the sweetest chocolate milk in the land." Local people love how we honor that legacy. We sell out of them every year.

We were one of the pioneers in reigniting the wine business in North Carolina. Today, the Yadkin Valley has over forty wine businesses. More importantly to me personally, the farm empowered our family to work together and play together as our children grew up. Yes, it took many years for the business to break even, but I would do it all over again if given the

> The farm empowered our family to work together and play together as our children grew up.

opportunity. And today the place is alive with great wines, food, and music, as well as walking trails that connect to the North Carolina Mountain-to-Seas Trail, a footpath stretching almost 1,200 miles across North Carolina from Clingmans Dome in the Great Smoky Mountains to Jockey's Ridge on the Outer Banks.

Now, here comes the commercial—you can find out more about the winery at www.grassycreekvineyard.com and the cabin rentals at www.theklondikecabins.com. And when you're visiting those websites, please appreciate how beautiful they are—my daughter, Caroline, built them!

CHAPTER 12

Empowered by
NEW CHALLENGES

We all have our mountains to climb throughout our lifetimes, both personally and professionally. And it always takes courage and perseverance to take the first step on those ascents. In this chapter, I want to share one of my most demanding ascents—in the literal sense of the word.

I've always sought out new challenges. They empower me to improve my skills, up my game, and go places where I've never been before. On a personal level, I've always had an unquenchable thirst for extreme and exciting sports adventures. As a result, I've experienced north-face back-mountain snow skiing in Crested Butte, Colorado, white water rafting on the Gully River, kayaking, sky diving, and much more. I've

> Empower me to improve my skills, up my game, and go places where I've never been before.

enjoyed doing all these activities, but after I turned fifty, I still had one left on my bucket list—rock climbing.

Lori knew I wanted to try it, so she gave me a book on rock climbing to get started. I began training while living in Shanghai. In that city, however, I could only use indoor climbing walls in the city proper as well as running with a weighted backpack up hills in parking lots—very limited training options. Still, I felt I was good to go. So I hired a private guide named Kevin, located in Nevada, and flew to Red Rock Canyon in that state for my long-awaited climbing adventure.

Kevin was a twenty-five-year-old lifter and former Netherlands professional soccer player. As I said, I was in my early fifties, so this was not going to be any kind of Sunday school picnic for me. Day one was basic training and practicing. Just the two of us trained on a mountain, and I learned very quickly how we had to depend on each other to stay safe—Kevin faked some falls to see if he could rely on me to stop him from falling to the bottom. Talk about a trust exercise— no wonder we became fast friends. We finished that first day with a two-hundred-foot climb on a preplanted anchor in the rock wall. My mood didn't change on the way up and the way back down—what I felt was constant fear and extreme exhaustion!

But I guess I hadn't done too badly. As we headed back to his office, Kevin said I was the best first-time climber he had ever guided. For our actual ascent, he selected a specific mountain nearby that would be perfect for my climbing adventure—my limited climbing skills could handle it, and it would provide some breathtaking views as well.

I was still hesitant. That day, as I said, we had gone two hundred feet straight up, and to me, that fulfilled my objective—I really didn't know if I could go beyond what we had just done, but I still left the door open. I told him if I wasn't at his office ready to go at 6:30 a.m. the next morning, I was out.

Yes, my courage was rapidly deserting me.

That evening, with the help of a Jack Daniels and Diet Coke, I got it back. The next morning, I was there and ready to take on the mountain. He drove us to where we would start the climb. We parked and began a swift ninety-minute hike into the depths of the mountain ranges. As we arrived at the base location, he announced, "Here we are!" Okay, then. After some gear reconfiguration—getting fresh water, changing our shoes, packing our anchor cams and carabiner clips, and putting on our helmets—we were ready to go. We also took along two-hundred-foot ropes, the distance for each leg of our forthcoming climb.

Kevin seemed to move like a spider monkey as he climbed and set the pace. Middle-aged me tried to keep up. About every ten feet, he would place an anchor cam in a rock crevice and snap it in. I gripped his safety line and watched closely—because if he fell off the rock, I was his only hope. Once he reached the two-hundred-foot mark, he gave me the prearranged signal, and we switched the rope configuration so he became my lifeline for my climb.

That was when my courage took a hike yet again. I stood staring up at the rock formation from the base of the mountain, feeling helpless. I was frozen with panic and couldn't find my first spot to place a toe or grab with my hand so I could begin my ascent. Finally, I took a deep breath, regrouped, and found my way up. At each ten-foot interval, I had to release the anchor cam, attach it to my belt, and then proceed to the next one. We would need to reuse them all on the next leg of the climb.

I had gotten up to around a hundred feet when I found myself struggling. I was already exhausted, and my resolve to keep going up the mountain weakened. I was far from being a seasoned climber—and, probably because I was a lifter, I relied on my upper-body strength more than I should have, rather than striking a balance between my lower and upper body. That resulted in me scratching and cutting up my shins, because I was making a habit of letting them drag along the side of the mountain.

So, as I hung there at that hundred-foot mark, I found myself asking what I thought was the most relevant question of that moment—*What in hell am I doing?* I had an amazing family and a great job. Okay, sure, I had plenty of life insurance, but that didn't offer me much comfort at the time. Frankly, dying wasn't on the agenda!

Up until that point, I had kept my eyes strictly focused upward as I continued to climb, constantly on the lookout for the next toe or finger hold. But at this particular moment, when I was questioning my sanity, I took a moment to look down over my shoulder and saw an amazing sight—the colors of the red rocks were streaming like a moving river of red. I could hear mountain goats in the distance. And I saw a hawk flying effortlessly through the air. All my senses were entranced by the wonderful scenery and nature all around me, and that gave me enough juice to recharge my motivation. I climbed the rest of the way up to where Kevin was waiting for me.

There, I tied myself off in such a way that I could pull my legs up to a horizontal squat position and lean back against the torque of the rope. I handed off the anchor cams to Kevin and grabbed a drink of water as Kevin asked me the inevitable question—"Are you up for climbing the next leg?"

I nodded my head.

We climbed three more legs of two hundred feet apiece. And each time at the halfway mark of each leg, I asked myself the same question as before—"What in hell am I doing?" Each time, I had to summon up my courage again and continue. We made it all the way to the top, where the view was truly breathtaking. I could see a whole range of mountain tops as far as the eye could see. There was not a cloud in the sky, and it felt like I could just reach up and touch heaven. It was a profoundly emotional moment for me that's hard to describe.

Luckily, a descent is much easier and faster than an ascent, as it just involves repelling down the wall of rock. However, it's just as dangerous, so safety protocols remained priorities to keep top of mind. At the bottom of the mountain, we packed up and started the ninety-minute hike back to the Jeep.

When we were about two hundred yards from the parking area, Kevin turned to me and said, "I usually turn it up from here and jog back to the Jeep. Are you up for it?" What could I say? I was not sure I had enough left in the tank to do that run, but I was determined not to wimp out after this overwhelming experience. "Yes," I replied, and off we went. When all was said and done, it had been a strenuous ten-hour day that felt like it was over in the blink of an eye.

Once we arrived at the Jeep, I was breathing hard like a fifty-something man does after all that. I reached into my bag inside the Jeep and pulled out what I thought was a well-earned cigarette—maybe not the best medicine when you're out of breath, but it sure hit the spot. After my first puff, I couldn't help but dream about enjoying a cold beer too. That's when Kevin pulled out a small cooler and said, "Hey, I'll trade you a Corona for a cig." Dreams do come true! That had to be the best beer of my life, as we leaned against the Jeep admiring the landscape and embracing our accomplishment.

That moment reminded me of a quote on a Marcus Pearson painting in my home office: "I have tasted victory and I have found it to be like wine. If it was produced without passion, was created haphazardly, and was easy to come by—the taste was hollow, unfulfilling, and it left behind a lingering bitterness. If, however, the victory was the end result of true commitment, careful preparation, and a love of the task—the taste was complex and lovely, both smooth and strong, like robust velvet. So gorgeous, and it finished with just a hint of … swagger."

As we traveled back to town, Kevin put in the latest Kings of Leon CD and played his favorite song on it, "Radioactive." I looked out the window to hide my tears of emotion, which were starting to roll down my face.

Courage and perseverance were the keys to completing my rock climb. I also reflected they were the keys to climbing our own personal mountains in our everyday lives. We may feel discouraged. We may feel we will fail. But we must keep putting one foot in front of the other to complete the all-important quests that bring us the kind of life experiences we're after.

To me, that's the secret to personal empowerment.

CHAPTER 13

Empowerment,
NOT ENABLEMENT

This is going to be a very short chapter.

As this book nears its ending, I want to acknowledge that there is a limit on how far you can empower someone else. Sometimes it just doesn't work, and there's nothing you can do about it.

I learned this from a difficult experience I once had with a friend and fellow lifter whom I had known for some twenty-five years. He was also an electrician I hired to do a lot of work on several properties of mine over the years. I know his former wife—a delightful woman. And one of his sons started his own landscaping business a few years back and currently handles all my yard work needs. So there was a close relationship there.

I don't know the root cause of this next chain of events—but I found it very troubling at the time. He divorced his wife. He became estranged from his children and grandchildren. He received back-to-back DUIs, causing him to lose his license to drive his commercial truck, and for a year, he spent weekends working off his resulting jail time. He also had been in at least two fist fights in local pubs. And finally, he began dating a young lady about half his age (I met her one afternoon at the gym, and she seemed very nice. But she was only twenty, and he was in his early fifties).

I learned most of this from local friends and acquaintances—apparently, he was the talk of the town because of all his misadventures. I could only shake my head and wonder what was going on with him.

Recently, I received a text message from him out of the blue asking me to give him a call. I hadn't talked to him in a couple of years, so I had to wonder what this was about. You might be ahead of me on this. Anyway, after a perfunctory back-and-forth catching up, he told me he needed a favor. He told me a dramatic story about his ex-wife embezzling money from his business account and how he was set to take her to court. The upshot was he needed a "bridge loan" because he had a $3,000 issue he needed to resolve and didn't have the money. He explained that he would, of course, sign proper paperwork to show he was serious about paying me back.

Well, if it was only $3,000, I wasn't going to go to the trouble of doing paperwork. I was all set to just provide him that amount, knowing I would probably never see that money again. However, I found out that wasn't what he was asking for. That was just the most pressing debt he had on his hands.

What he was asking for was *$30,000.*

Wow. I told him to send me some copies of the bills he was behind on and I would think about it. He did so and I talked to his creditors. He did owe all this money. He sure wasn't kidding about that.

However, I also had to think about how the construction business was booming. It took six months just to get a quote from an electrician at the time, because they were all so busy. His skills had to be in serious demand. At the same time, I kept seeing pictures of frequent, lavish vacations he was taking that he posted on Facebook. And everything I heard about what he was up to didn't inspire my confidence—he obviously had some very serious life issues that he wasn't dealing with. It was not a question of whether or not I *could* give him the money. What I was asking myself is *should* I give him the money?

I deliberated with a heavy heart. I talked with close friends about my dilemma, and I prayed about it as well. Would giving him the money be empowering him through a tough time? Or would it in fact be enabling him to continue turning his life topsy-turvy without making a genuine attempt to get things back on track? I stressed over this for days because I truly wanted to help a friend—but I also did not want to make things worse for him by throwing kerosene on the fire of his less-than-desirable choices.

I finally decided to say no. I felt as though he was putting all his problems on my doorstep and expecting a big wad of money from me to magically make them disappear. When I talked to him again, I told him to consider stopping all the vacations. I told him to focus on what was really driving his current dysfunction. I made the point that if he didn't, he would just be back in a few months asking for more money. I hoped he would find the path forward.

And I hope I did the right thing.

I am sad to say my friend died not long after that, in a strange and unexpected way. He got into yet another bar fight and was beaten pretty badly. A few days later, he was playing catch with his dog in his backyard. When the authorities reviewed the security camera footage, all that could be seen was him losing his balance, passing out, and falling into his pool. However, there was no fluid in his lungs, so he had to have died before he hit the water. The doctors said it was either a heart attack or some kind of brain aneurysm that killed him.

Would $30,000 have prevented that from happening? I don't see how. He had already lost a lot of business because of his hard partying, and the bar fight was another in a string of difficult times he had brought on himself. Still, I grieved over the loss of someone who was once a great friend. I just wish he could've found a way to empower himself to a life-changing recovery.

People can lose the plot in a number of ways. One of the biggest problems plaguing our society these days is addiction, which is defined as a neuropsychological disorder characterized by a persistent and intense urge to use or do something, despite substantial harm and other negative consequences.

> My advice is, when faced with a situation involving addiction (whether it's you or someone you know), choose the route of empowerment, not enablement.

Addiction comes in many forms. Many of us may have some sort of addiction that can lead to a dependency on not just drugs or alcohol but also sex, money, work, workouts, and more. There are several ways to deal with addictions. Some choose to manage them through moderation. Some choose to abstain from them altogether. And some choose to seek help and support.

My advice is, when faced with a situation involving addiction (whether it's you or someone you know), choose the route of empowerment, not enablement. When you keep feeding a snake, it can grow big enough to eat you. Same with an addiction. When you can't control it, it ends up controlling you. The only way to break free is to admit there is a problem and seek a viable solution. Follow the path that will bring you out of your self-destructive ways, and you will find peace through that journey.

I wish my friend had.

Some Final Thoughts on
EMPOWERMENT

I hope you've enjoyed my stories of empowerment. And trust me, my story's not over yet. Yes, I'm getting older, but I'm not ready to be put out to pasture yet. I really enjoyed my last experience running a company for a private equity firm, and so I have accepted a position as CEO of API Heat Transfer. I'm excited to once again build a great team and empower an organization to do amazing things.

Now, I want to wrap this book up by making a few more important points about the concept of empowerment.

First of all, listening is a crucial ingredient of any empowerment effort.

To effectively empower a team or an individual, you must first listen to the needs of that team or individual. To effectively empower personal relationships, such as those with family members, you must also listen to them and acknowledge their feelings. What works for you may not work for them. That's where listening comes into play—because that's how you learn about others and what makes them tick.

Otherwise, it's like you're playing poker blindfolded. You can't know what card to play or when, so you could easily lose out on building productive relationships.

Listening is a skill mastered by few. Most people aren't really listening in a conversation—they're too busy quietly thinking about what their response is going to be. In the words of the great author Stephen Covey, "Listen with the intent to understand, not with the intent to reply."

And by the way, listening isn't just about verbal communication; it's also about nonverbal communication. Sometimes, you can spot an expression or a gesture that signals what someone is really thinking, and it can be at odds with what's coming out of their mouth. For example, someone might tell you they're on board with what you're saying, but you might see something in their eyes that indicates they're hesitant or afraid to express how they're really feeling. That's your cue to do some gentle probing of their actual opinions.

The problem is that listening is too often regarded as a passive process. It shouldn't be. It's actually an *active* process, where you're working to take in what the other person is communicating rather than thinking about what you're going to have for dinner that night or whatever else is distracting you at the moment.

My second point about empowerment is it also demands leadership skills. I took many classes on the subject over the years, but I wanted to take a moment to salute the program that really empowered me to be the best leader possible. That program is the Thayer Leadership program, inspired by Sylvanus Thayer, the "Father of West Point," and led by retired colonels and generals, who teach classes on the actual West Point campus. As I mentioned earlier, when I was CEO of PCI, I joined the Manufacturing Association of Plastic Processors, where I was named to its board of directors and eventually became VP of the association. Well, as a group, we decided to look for a leadership program that would benefit all of us in this particular industry. This was the one we chose, and they tailored the program to our specific needs.

Many have called business a game of war. Well, actual war is no "game." We learned that pretty quickly when the Thayer instructors told us stories about the demands placed on leaders during actual combat. We heard some pretty hair-raising accounts where it was a matter of life and death. Business is tough but not that tough. It's a different kind of war, where we're in a constant battle not only against our competition but also to overcome challenges like attracting talent and retaining it successfully, supply chain issues, industry disruptors, new technology, and so forth. The army uses an acronym to describe a battlefield environment—VUCA, which stands for *volatile, uncertain, complex, ambiguous*. Those terms also definitely describe the issues we face in business, especially these days.

How can a leader most effectively handle the VUCA of business? Well, one of our exercises at the Thayer program was to craft our own personal leadership statement. I was very happy with the results, and I'd like to share that statement, which is contained in the graphic below:

| PERSONAL LEADERSHIP STATEMENT |

APPRECIATION
- Recognize, Reward, Thank You
- Treat Others as You Would Treat Yourself
- Respect
- Relationship Building

SERVICE
- Servant Leadership
- Empower, Enable
- Learn from Failure
- Humility
- Balance—Work, Family, Faith

STRATEGY
- Vision and Direction
- Establish the Intent and Purpose of the Mission
- Development, Learning

EXCELLENCE
- Hard Work
- Passion
- Sense of Urgency
- Courage and Resilience

ACCOUNTABILITY/TEAMWORK
- Work as a Team—Hold Self Accountable
- Responsibility
- Integrity
- Loyalty
- Lead by Example

Finally, my third and last point concerns what I believe to be the ultimate source of empowerment—faith and God.

The term *civilization* may not be the best term to describe humankind. We have a bloody and savage history that includes the Vikings (not the football team), Genghis Khan and his barbarian hordes, European explorers conquering the native population of North America, Hitler and World War II, and ongoing racism and discrimination. Currently, we face similar geopolitical chaos that's causing global suffering and death. So I don't know how "civilized" we really are.

However, it's never too late, and I do believe we can be empowered to change the world in a positive way if we follow the Word of the Lord, who offers a source for comfort, a path to salvation, and so much more. I don't want to oversell my own religious convictions—I have never been disciplined enough to practice prayer on a daily basis, for example. But when I have a family member or friend in need, or when I lack direction or feel a personal burden, I do pray—and God has always responded to me in some fashion or form.

Evan Almighty is a delightful movie that stars Steve Carell as Evan (a modern-day Noah); Lauren Graham as his wife, Joan; and Morgan Freeman as God, a role he's very well suited for. If you haven't seen it, here's the plot: Evan is called by God to build a new ark in modern-day America, because another epic flood is coming. Joan thinks Evan's going a little nutty and takes off with their sons. They go to a sandwich shop, where the boys go to the restroom. That's when Morgan Freeman, disguised as a bus boy, joins her at a table where she's sitting by herself. They have the following conversation.

Joan: My husband says God told him to build it. What do you do with that?

God: Sounds like an opportunity. Let me ask you something. If someone prays for patience, do you think God will give them patience? Or does he give them the opportunity for patience? If someone prays for courage, does God give them courage? Or does God give them the opportunity for courage? If someone prays for the family to be close, does God daze them with warm and fuzzy feelings? Or does he give them opportunities to love each other?

In other words, if you believe God is going to magically change you or your life without you having to do the work, that's not going to happen. God opens doors for us. It's up to us to walk through them.

I could burden you with endless thoughts reflecting my superficial understanding of such intangibles as abstract geometry, quirk theory, multidimensional universes, black hole theory, Einstein's theory of relativity, and the implications of the wall presented by the speed of light (I will always be a big fan of Steven Hawking, as well as a follower of *Star Trek*—my tattoos can attest to that!) and try to get closer to whatever God is. However, I think another approach is to ask a seemingly simple question—why does man have no real idea how the human brain works? It's the most powerful information processing tool at the lowest cost of energy we know of, and we have not yet been able to duplicate its overall power.

A few months ago, I sat by a young lady with a PhD in neuroscience who worked for a very large medical company. And I posed that exact question. Her response was that we are gaining a real understanding of cause and effect within a brain—but the fact is that we have made no real progress on determining how our minds truly work (she suggested I read the book *A Molecule Away from Madness*, by Sara Manning Peskin, to gain more insight). I think there's a reason for that, and that reason has to do with our spiritual sides.

I cannot gaze into the sky and not believe that there is more to this universe than our so-called rational minds can ever understand. The mere fact the Bible has remained in some form of existence for over two thousand years must cause you to ask how and why this could happen. That is where faith comes in. Faith inspires us to trust, to believe, and to be comforted. Faith is the true and most powerful source of empowerment.

But again, we must meet faith halfway by doing our own work on ourselves. Unless we approach our lives and our loved ones in a positive and productive way, faith alone won't do the job.

I introduced you to a very influential mentor in my life earlier in this book—Tony Raffo, the three-hundred-pound Italian. He would regularly shout in his deep voice, "Attitudes are contagious—is yours worth catching?" He believed you had two choices when you enter a room—do you brighten it or darken it?

Similarly, *Evan Almighty* begins and ends with God asking a question and then finally providing an answer.

God: How do we change the world?

Evan: One single act of random kindness at a time.

God: [writing A-R-K on the ground with a stick] One … Act … of Random Kindness … at a time.

Now, as I enter the final pages of this book, I'd like to suggest you ask yourself a few questions to determine the level of your own personal empowerment:

1. Do you practice servant leadership with empowerment as your foundation?

2. Who has empowered you over the years? Are you paying that empowerment forward?

3. In Tony's words, is your attitude worth catching?

I truly hope you enjoyed the read and learned that you, too, can reap the benefits of true empowerment, as I have throughout my life.

Best,

Derrill

About the Author

Derrill Rice is a seasoned executive with a significant record of extracting value in building and rebuilding businesses, whether it is a start-up, a turn-around, or when scaling for growth. He has led organizations across a range of industries and has extensive operating experience with plant construction and market development in multiple countries as well as technical expertise resulting in patent awards. He is valued for his ability to lead in multicultural environments and to integrate diverse cultures. He is a player/coach, collaborator, and strong communicator who engages, aligns, and directs a team to exceed expectations. Prioritizing safety, customer engagement, effective communications, and creating value, Derrill leads with empowerment as a foundation to servant leadership. He loves to win and celebrate success but also enjoys the journey of competition and learning from any setbacks. Finally, he has a foundation of integrity and an attitude of commitment that has earned significant respect from colleagues, peers, and friends.

Derrill has held the titles of CEO, president, division president, senior vice president, general manager, business manager, and plant manager in multiple textile, electronic, and industrial manufacturing sectors. He holds an MBA from Clemson University, Summa Cum

Laude, and a BS in Business from Presbyterian College, Summa Cum Laude. And he serves as a board member, advisor, and CEO coach on several fronts.

Derrill is married to an educational professional passionate about gifted education, early childhood development, interactive classrooms, and teaching teachers. Their two young adult children are pursuing careers in marketing and engineering.

Acknowledgments

*To those who played important roles in
my journey of servant leadership:*

The People

- Tim Wilson—Best friend since seventh grade, accomplished comedian, and artist, who departed too early in his time with all of us here!

- Windle McKenzie—Math teacher, coach, headmaster, and one who has made such a positive difference in so many young lives!

- David Spitzmiller—A football legend in every regard, especially to me!

- Tony Raffo—A bigger-than-life Italian who defines the importance of attitude and has inspired so many!

- Joe Gorga—A boss, a friend, and a colleague for half of my career—you are missed by many!

- Steve Merkt—Simply a leader of unparalleled excellence in every regard!

- Mike Hargett—The smartest person and fastest mind I have ever known!

- Joyce Moore—An underappreciated anchor through so many storms!

- Jim Douthit—A business partner turned family member!

- Robin Smith and Todd Scearce—Weightlifting and Harley Davidson brothers from other mothers!

- Lily Zhou—Inspiration and empowerment from the most unexpected places!

- Durwood Williams—From nothing to amazing, and the best hands-on operations leader of all times!

The Institutions

- Brookstone Highschool—"We'll teach them to be the one with bold ideas."

- Kappa Alpha Order—A brotherhood that lasts a lifetime and "a moral compass for the modern gentleman."

- Presbyterian College—"America's Innovative Service College."

- Superflex Gym—Where the big boys move weight like it was a religion!

- Thayer Leadership/West Point—Where leadership can make the difference between life and death!

And Most Importantly—Immediate Family

- Jane Page Shoemaker—My mother, who demonstrated the power of faith and the commitment to what is important—family! I so do love you!

- Alan Rice—My younger brother, best friend, world's best air guitar player, and spiritual compass!

- My immediate family—Lori, Caroline, and Austin—Unwavering support, excellence beyond any possible expectations, valuing our most precious resource—time—and the reason I charge forward every day! I "married up"!

CPSIA information can be obtained
at www.ICGtesting.com
Printed in the USA
JSHW021459050523
41312JS00001B/11